How to be the Boss of Your Own Money

A Guide to Better Mind & Money Management

PATRICIA OGILVIE

PATRICIA OGILVIE

Published by ProRisk Press

Box 253, Alberta Beach, Alberta, Canada

T0E 0A0

Patricia@auntisays.com

AuntiSays.com

Copyright © 2017 Patricia Ogilvie

Cover Design © 2017
Cover Designed by Prorisk Press

Stock images from GraphicStock

All rights reserved. No part of this publication may be reproduced or transmitted in any form or by any means, including informational storage and retrieval systems, without permission in writing from the copyright holder, except for brief quotations in a review.

ISBN-13: 978-1979384308

ISBN-10: 1979384304

The Art of Money Getting

CONTENTS

Preface	1
Introduction	6
What Length Would You Take	21
Phases of Prosperity	27
Debt is a Delicate Subject	46
Effortless Budgets	49
13 Best Money Saving Practices	66
How to Have It All	80
Conclusion	94
More About Patricia	98

ACKNOWLEDGMENTS

To my friends and family who supported me writing and writing and loving me along the way.

PREFACE

Imagine for a second that most of the money that runs through your fingers, stays with you, stays in your bank account.

Can you imagine this? I hope so, because when you believe it, those thoughts and corresponding feelings about money are the glue that either supports you to keep money or retreat from it. What if each time you are asked about or reminded about money, the first notion that pops into your head is, money flows through me like a bad case of diarrhea.

Too graphic? That's how a friend of mine believed about money. Shitty and loose. So, I wrote this book to help her change that mental image. I'm hoping it may change your perspective about money.

I could have called this "The Top-Secret Ways to Reprogram Your Subconscious Gremlins And Become Debt Free and Retirement Rich".

That was too long.

I understand you want more money. I know you want more of it to stay with you for later years and be available to you in lean times.

So truthfully this book should be entitled "The Art of Money Getting and Keeping".

It's simply named "Be The Boss of Your Own Money."

How would you feel if this were possible and easier than you thought?

You may or may not know that I have decades of financial experience. Many of you are asking for help how to earn better money.

Did you see that? "Better instead of more". There's a difference and we'll cover that in this book. I can take you from frustration to a level of confidence so you have a positive feeling of control over money instead of it having a negative consequence control over you.

First, let me qualify that I too had financial issues at one time. I came from meager beginnings. We didn't have money, but we had a massive garden, a pen of chickens and cultivated love for adventure on my parents' farm in Northern Alberta Canada.

And we did better when my parents worked two jobs each. As I became an adult, my own bottom line wasn't always in the black as it is now. Years ago, my husband and I were almost $200,000 in debt at one point and needless to say, our relationship was strained.

Maybe you feel the strain with debt? Maybe it is affecting your relationships and everything else in your life? You are not alone. It's prevalent across the world.

You may have heard: at the recent World Summit, one of the candidates said eighty-five people hold more money among themselves than all the other 2 billion people in the rest of the world. Incredible, isn't it? But I'm not among the eighty-five, just so you'd know.

However, I did come from strong roots to work hard, was educated and for that I am grateful. In fact, I took the Canadian Securities course just so I could learn about investments, strategies and why money does what it does. I wanted to learn about how to keep and grow better money.

Just because I went this route to prepare myself for my future retirement, doesn't mean you have to. In fact, it's easier than you might think it is to live well, retire well and stop stressing once and for all.

Even though I enjoyed "books" and "figures', which gave me the incentive to learn what was good and what was bad debt, you don't have to follow my path. If you read this one book and do the steps I outline, you will begin to make a difference in your financial dream. You can do this a day at a time. In fact, there are 21 days of action steps here. And habits are busted in about 21 days.

Let me be honest here. Over the years, the conventional standards to make money, to keep money, and stay out of debt didn't always work for me, and not even at times for the rich and famous.

In fact, the most notoriously wealthy real estate tycoon, Donald Trump, who we all know is now the POTUS, made and lost over a billion dollars because of the decisions he made. There are many more who have come from humble to rich and back to humble beginnings because something within had them struggling.

I vowed not to have this happen to me. I soon discovered how to bust the debt habit and grow my bank account. Now I want to help you achieve freedom from the trap of debt. Here's one of the biggest learning I would love to impart to you; money is a metaphor for attention.

If that shakes you up, good. You see, so many of your actions are for gaining attention. And most of those actions are programmed decisions you made at an early age that keep replaying and replaying without your ever needing to know why.

Many of your actions are unconscious. You can get confused especially when you want to make a change in your lifestyle. Yet, nothing changes because, your internal recorder is playing out your life decisions and choices over and over. That internal runs your life.

In other words, you have literally another brain. It's the unconscious niggling that you learned as a child. It's the unconscious thought process that eggs you on to make good or bad decisions based on what you learned as a child. And despite her only being 8 or 10 years old when you learned something about money, you follow her advice. You follow the advice of a child when it comes to making financial decisions.

INTRODUCTION

"Grab a brain!" I used to hear this a bit even in my own home. I laugh because I know precisely what was happening and with whom when the phrase was suggested. I think you can relate.

However, what I'm suggesting is we should use the phrase "Grow a brain!" instead. Our brains are intricate learning tools, and if not kept limbered with open-mindedness and eagerness to find out more about how to live better lives, we will suffer with loneliness, desperation, debt and fear.

Avoiding responsibility of developing new brain capabilities keeps us repeating past patterns, and blocks us from becoming more creative and conscious of better lives, better money.

In other words, if you want to change you have to change your brain. In order to do that, you have to keep expanding your experiences. Ask good questions. You know yourself. Or do you?

Hi, I'm Patricia Ogilvie, and I want to help you reduce debt traditionally, but also using the most powerful tools in modern coaching systems, applying unconventional secrets to clearing debt and rebuilding better results. I am certified as an energy coach and have two University advanced degrees in administration and finance. I built my own retirement nest egg and now joyfully live with zero debt. I want to share some of the tricks, tips and secrets because you may want to grow old financially well.

Right now, I want to help you discover this little know secret to erasing debt and allowing more money to stay in your bank account. My precious nieces and nephews poke fun at me every time I say to them, sock away 10%. Even if you find a $20 bill on the street, put 10% away. That's the main secret.

But don't stress, because before getting to the saving part, that debt habit must be dealt with. If I'm being totally honest, society today has so many options and so much stuff tempting us, it is difficult to keep the cash in the pocket, to keep the credit card at bay, and to stop incurring debt. Some people truly have difficulty living within their means.

Why is it so difficult to live within means? Why does it seem frustrating to save and invest for the future? Simple. It's a habit - a bad habit. A habit is a lie you tell yourself in your head and in your heart over and over until you decide it has truth and validity. And even though you decide to tell yourself a different story, the old one keeps on playing out despite your best efforts.

The majority thinks that if they make more money they can pay off their debts and they will be happier. The reality is, that's a big fat lie. And it's run by a decision you made in your earliest memory about whether you deserved to be rich or whether you deserved instead to live a frustrated lifestyle. In fact, you may have borrowed that 'poor' thinking and planning from someone you looked up to.

It doesn't matter how much money you bring in, if you don't deal with the underlying habit of creating debt, you will just get in deeper and deeper and deeper. Even rich people can be dramatically in debt.

Marrying rich isn't going to help either! Here's something else you may have noticed. This theme replays itself over social media waves. If you're on Facebook and Twitter, you see this everyday on the threads. People are frustrated that they don't have enough money to support themselves and their families. They want opportunities to earn more and I don't blame them because truthfully, life costs.

I'll tell you right now, it doesn't matter if you get more money, unless you first break the habit of creating debt. Debt's replaying pattern will continue and all that happens is the debt becomes bigger.

Well, if not bigger, definitely rooted, planted and solidly stuck in you until the day you die. That's leaving a legacy of dread, isn't it? When you earn more money, what happens is you wind up spending more because there is more.

So here you are. What to do? Keep reading.

I challenge you to take your chances and make some financial management changes in the next month.

Picture this: you've graduated college; you're 25 years old and have just received the first significant bonus of your blossoming career.

What's the first thing you do? You try to figure out how you might spend the money: should you travel or go on a shopping spree? Take in a weekend music festival with friends?

On the other hand, (hopefully) you may be thinking about making a dent in the debt you've accumulated--or even considering putting a portion away to benefit your financial future. So, whom can you turn to for solid financial advice?

That's what I thought. You don't trust the status quo. You rely on your parents to steer you in the correct direction that would make the best impact on your financial future.

What if they don't know or are poor financial managers? This lack of trust could be an indication that you want to be more independent and prefer making your own money decisions. You learned from them all the same.

Again, I understand. I was like you too. But let's both admit, we worry about our financial future at least once a week or more, suggesting peace of mind is not a universal trait. I broke that habit a long time ago. And I'll show you how.

But first, if you're a woman, and correct me if I'm wrong about you, you probably tend to be less confident than your male counterparts about money. How do I know? I was you at one time.

I also did some research to qualify what I'm saying. Fidelity Mutual did a Millennial and Money study that revealed as many as 39% of young people worry about finances and, get this, one in four don't know who to trust. Neil Howe and William Strauss, authors of the 1991 book Generations: The History of America's Future, 1584 to 2069, is often credited with coining the term millennial. Howe and Strauss define them as individuals born between 1982 and 2004.

Fidelity Mutual surveyed them and wrote that 19% of millennial men said they never worry about their financial security, whereas only 2 percent of women can say the same.

"Feeling financially 'on their own' about finances also could be fallout from the Great Recession, since many Gen Y-ers witnessed their parents and grandparents struggle with the impact of job losses, tighter budgets, and/or declining retirement accounts," says Kristen Robinson, senior vice president, Fidelity Investments.

"Whatever the reason, this generation fortunately has a big advantage--the luxury of time, as nothing is more powerful than the impact of saving early and often."

And that's why I want you to grab and hold tight. You have time on your hands. If you're older, you can still capture your financial freedom dream, maybe not as much put away, but a significant amount so you too can feel better about yourself.

If you're serious about reducing debt and thinking long-term by taking steps to save early, you have options like 401(k) and RRSP's as well as having an IRA. If you're in earnest to tackle and place "accumulate more for retirement" at the top of your life list, you will be financially secure.

On the flip side, the research by Fidelity also indicated that many don't have money in a 401(k) and this is cause for concern. This means some who have access to a 401(k) or workplace plan aren't taking advantage of the "free money" on the table in the form of a company match from their employer, as well as the related financial guidance available through a workplace plan.

As an accountant for a retailer here in my home city, the staff almost felt offended when I recommended they invest a portion of their wages into the RRSP investment program. Getting free money wasn't a benefit. Surprised? Their basis in truth was that they just get by. And putting some away even if it grows for the long term doesn't meet the present term obligations.

Professionals suggest saving 10 percent to 15 percent of one's annual pay for retirement, inclusive of both personal and workplace contributions.

"This trend toward saving is encouraging, especially since the oldest of this generation are now juggling competing demands, such as saving to buy a house, raising a family or starting a college fund for their own children," says Robinson.

"Finding ways to turn positive savings habits into more deliberate investing strategies can make a huge difference--and may provide the peace of mind many millennials desire."

What Fidelity found and I did as well, people either didn't understand or don't trust to part with their money to allow it to grow for them.

There are tools, videos and a wealth of resources targeted to people at the early stages of their investing lives, helping them transition ideas into actions. Tools include budgeting spreadsheets, helpful articles and step-by-step guidance on saving and investing.

LinkedIn Influencer Kathy Murphy's "If I Were 22 – Get a Financial Head Start" discusses the importance of charting your savings goals and setting aside more starting at an early age. If I were 22 again, I'd get my head screwed on tighter and seek out some professional financial advice. Hindsight, you know?

You don't have to part with your money until and unless you completely trust and understand what you are planning to do with it. Listen, even if right now, you are in debt, you can still be happy. This survey says that important feeling good aspects include relief when you could see a loan or credit card value reduce right in front of your eyes. Pretty awesome, isn't it?

Personal finance is about setting yourself life goals. Being frugal while you're young means you can have a wonderful life in your mid and later years. But if you're not young, you can still plan for the future.

It's all up to you. For example, spend on things that matter. That extra latte or lunch out isn't supporting your long-term vision. Ask yourself the most important question. "What is it you want?"

What if you could save 10% or more for your retirement right now? What if you could be guaranteed saving a down payment on the house of your dreams? What if you had an emergency fund of 3-6 months if the economy turned down?

What if even in a down turned time you had a reserve to take a trip without worry? Or get married? Or have a child? Or take another class? Or? You decide. What would motivate you to stay away from bad debt and make good income increasing decisions? What is your heart's content? Would you like to know the first clue?

Balance.

Oh sure, the term balance is overused and overrated. What's your definition of balance? Allow me to share mine. Balance is a mental construct of not being obsessed with money and financial security, but not ignoring it either.

Knowing what balance means to you, you can begin the journey to your own financial freedom. Because your thoughts create your reality and your thoughts about money, why not create a viable reality with your money? That's why I wrote this for you.

You see, the less attention you pay to your finances now, the more likely you are to be plagued by time-consuming financial difficulties later. The less attention you pay to managing your money proactively, the more time and energy money matters are likely to consume in your life.

You can't avoid money. You know this. Money is a powerful force in your life whether you want it to be or not. There is no escaping it. By investing some time and effort in understanding how to use money effectively to support your life goals, and by developing good money management habits, you are more likely to end up having far fewer money worries.

That's what this book is about. You will go deeper and gain understanding to untangle those pesky gremlin beliefs that keep you tied down and stuck in your current financial situation.

What this book won't do is get you completely out of debt instantly. No. That journey takes a bit longer, even years. However, what I will guarantee this book will do for you is that if you do the work, you will stop incurring more bad debts. Instead, you will begin to feel a tingle of passion to reduce your current debt and begin to appreciate having more come in.

The intention is for you to release the habit of incurring debt and that can happen in days. How to break a habit? More importantly, how do you reprogram a belief that keeps you on the same rut over and over and over?

Personally, I have released a habit of going into fear and doubt in less than four days. When I smoked, I broke that habit in 2 weeks and haven't had a desire for a cigarette for over 20 years.

When I wanted to completely quit drinking wine, I did it in 4 hours!

I have helped dozens of people come to terms with realizing that some of the things they say and do are in fact just a habit they've become accustomed to over the years. It is MY desire to help you.

Are you ready stop the destructive habit of incurring debt no matter how much money you have? Please say yes. This book features a step-by-step process to change your mind, shift your thoughts, and you learn to enjoy yourself without spending the money you don't have.

This process will not only change the way you treat your money, it could end up changing the size of your bank account. If you'd like to join me, turn the page.

You are in for a treat. You will receive tips and suggestions, energy processing meditation exercises, and challenges, yes, challenges to become aware and shift out of the grip the habit to spend has on you.

Beware. This is for you if you are open minded and not faint of heart. Let me give you an example right here. Because if you grasp this concept now, you will enjoy the journey in front of you.

To create a financial surge in cash flow, you must first remove all internal and external money blocks. You see, debt is actually a block and it represents both internal and external. Debt is a block you decided a long time ago served you in some way. And because it's ingrained and repeats itself without you even knowing, it will be a challenge to find it. Oh yes, it sure will be because for one thing, it's not easily found. She hides.

You don't see it, you can't hear it, it doesn't talk back to you, it's just a recording playing over and over and over directing your life and decisions without you evening realizing it. An example of an internal block is simply a thought pattern that pops up each time you look at a pair of designer shoes. The thought is "they're too expensive but I don't care!" Or "I'll probably regret this later but oh well, you only live once!" Or, "I'm so upset right now, I need to buy this to feel better!"

The external block is more obvious. It's the near maxed out credit card you are forever paying minimum payments. You know you are paying abhorrent interest on minimum payments, right? Or a depleted bank account that may or may not cover the next month's expenses. It's the lifestyle of living pay cheque to pay cheque with no relief on the horizon that feels crappy and sucks out your energy big time.

I am so excited you are joining me throughout these pages of delicious ideas and energy shifting actions. Here are a few more pointers for you to remember:

1. Be prepared with an open mind about debt and the habit that could be destroying the very foundation you say you want.

2. Write in the borders of this book. If you're reading this online, grab a pen and paper and jot down ideas and notes as they pop up.

3. Bring a great attitude and get ready to dig deeper than ever about what makes you tick around money, debt and relationship. Let me reiterate: Attitude is the most important factor in determining your financial success or failure. Boom! (mike drop)

4. You're going to learn how to navigate some inner beliefs you might not be aware of yet, outer actions to increase your esteem, build confidence and boldly step up to grab what is rightfully yours without creating more frustrating debt.

5. The best part is you will finally meet those pesky gremlin beliefs that want to keep you in the same pattern for the rest of your life. And that's not what you want, is it? What you want is to stop the recording and hit the new play button to put in some new and exciting habits that will reduce debt and increase wealth.

How does that sound? Just a reminder, I'm not going to focus on how to increase your income or even how to keep the same income which "could" sustain you, yet. Nope. That will come soon enough.

In this first section, we're going to cover aspects of your habit of spending what you don't have. You're going to be challenged in your body, mind, spirit and relationships. This unique brand of steps and 21 days of activity and formula offers results-oriented lessons for a lifetime of financial confidence.

LET'S GET STARTED

For those who don't know me, here's a little about my talents and strengths so you don't think I'm coming from out of left field with this money getting stuff. As a 20-year veteran of accounting, tax preps, guiding online business start-ups, and a life and financial management coach for folks just like you, I would typically offer technical and business experience along with practical ways to market oneself to earn more money. Over the years, I noticed a pattern with my clients; many carried a larger than usual debt ratio to income. This situation made their personal lives frustrating and unfocussed about what they wanted to achieve.

In turn, this frustration translated into their professional lives and that negative energy popped up in unusual ways in their personal and professional relationships. What they didn't see was that their own clients are aware when something isn't quite right. Realizing this was one of the best lessons to making an immediate shift in perception.

I did something more for them and began to coach, guide and show my clients how to reduce the bad debt habit before continuing the business of earning more income. And it paid off.

As a financial accountant, Canadian Securities Commission trained in stock investments and within the past 5 years, an energy reading life coach, my specialty is in helping people balance their budgets and tackle debt with personalized plans by digging deeper into the subconscious reasons as to why the debt grows.

I began my financial career as an adult education instructor for accounting and bookkeeping programs. When we moved to the west coast, I shifted my career from teaching to coaching and now, for more than 10 years, I delve deep into the psychology and power of money. I have 2 advanced degrees in administration and retail finance. I teach adults financial management and support hundreds of debt ridden people to release the tension and frustration.

As the owner, founder and president of ProRisk Enterprises Ltd, I am also an author of 10 books including my personal favourite, "Please God, Don't Let Me Be a Bag Lady!" You can find the books on my website at auntisays.com

I take pride in the fact that my company conducts business in ways that honor the foundation I believe in: balanced, proud and profitable. I have spent more than two decades working successfully in finance and teaching, have achieved 6 figure financial goals in my personal and professional life. My husband of 33 years and I have no debt.

My skills include curriculum development in adult education environments, programs for school kids, and recently, a powerful online program to bust through the debilitating bad habit of debt. In addition to empowering and equipping my online audience with fresh takes on how to achieve Financial Freedom and stress release, I enjoy spending time with my husband Randy on our beautiful acreage overlooking Lac

The Art of Money Getting

Ste Anne in the interior of Alberta, Canada. (about 45 minutes from West Edmonton Mall)

And now, in these next sections, I'm going to show you that making more money along with reducing your current debt doesn't have to be freaky scary.

One of my clients went from excessive debt to attracting the ideal job and selling what needed to be sold to begin the process in earnest. You see, people, especially in their mid to later years are feeling stressed they may not get out of debt in time to enjoy the remainder years of their lives. I'm here to show you that it can be done - starting today. Here's Susan's story:

"In the beginning of your program I was about the 40 mark out of 100 which was too high on your ladder of intensity and fear of having too much debt. I came to realize that we had always relied on that pay cheque, never saved a nickel, blew it all on toys and leather furniture. Did we really need it? No. I look at others who pay themselves first, and their mortgage and vehicles are paid off. They aren't one's going after the toys, but now have that security that we want. We did the work! Fast forward to now and your Debt Challenge Program.

Yes, it all came to a crunch. Sitting down and hitting it head on was there. I did not want to answer the phone and talk to creditors. I do now. And I tell them the truth. It will now take us two years of steady payments to get back our AAA credit ratings. Do I want another credit card? Nope. Paying with cash and being more accountable. Even Debit/Visa is a pain as we swipe and swipe and not see it going out of the account as paper money does out of hand."

What Susan has experienced is that even with a little helping hand to find the financial leaky holes and patch them, she and her husband can recover nicely and move forward towards their financial freedom goals. Frankly, the small and more reasonable the financial goal you set, the more likely you are going to achieve it. (Keep this little tidbit tip in your back pocket for future reference.)

Ready to find your financial freedom? Ultimately, what you're going to read in this book is going to set you free. I'm going to streamline the process of getting your head screwed on tighter so you can make smarter decisions when it comes to money. And without you having to do a lot of extra work, because you already know what you need to do, try to enjoy the process.

WHAT LENGTH WOULD YOU TAKE?

First, let's ask the hard questions. What length would you take to survive financially? To what length would you go to reduce debt or increase earnings?

To what length would you be willing to take ownership of your own financial situation? What would you do for money?

I was originally going to share this next story with you at the end. But I actually thought you wouldn't get to the end soon enough for me! (Laughing at myself!)

It's an old story and it's a lesson in understanding that when push comes to shove, even the raw, wretched and demeaning could be tapped for fortune and piety.

In the ancient book, "The Twenty-Four Paragons of Filial Piety", by the Yuan Dynasty scholar Guo Jujing, is the story of a son who honored his aging father.

Long time ago, there was a scholar named Chûjun. His wife had died young, leaving him with three sons. His sons got married and had babies. One day the scholar gathers his three sons, and talks to them without witness:

I'm getting very old, my teeth are all fallen, and all that I can absorb now is milk, just like a baby. I would like to know which one of you three is the most pious son. The elder and younger brothers shout, that's me! No one is more pious than I am. The third said nothing. The old man said, I wish that the wife of one of you gives up her baby and let me suck the milk of the youngster.

The elder said, certainly not mine. And the younger, neither mine. The third said, children, I may have some others, but I have only one father, and I cannot replace him. My wife will give him the breast, and we abandon the brat.

The father orders him to dig a hole in a precise location at the foot of three pine trees. The pious son digs there and finds a treasure, which is a reward for his filial piety.

Are you willing to do whatever it takes to earn respect, piety, and possibly security?

I dislike this story because of the connotation a woman has no say. And I dislike any story that has anyone groveling for attention, which also means for the next dollar bill to keep afloat in today's fast paced world. Here's what I suggest instead: You avoid debt.

Are you surprised this is the number one premise of better financial management? Most people actually believe that having more money is the key to Financial Freedom. But that's a myth. Reducing and eliminating debt is actually the only way to the journey of self-sufficiency and freedom.

Here's why you should avoid running into debt.

There is nothing else in the whole world that drags a person down like debt. It has a slavish position to get in, yet so many, especially young people hardly out of school, are running in debt.

How does this happen? There's the cost of education to be sure. Then there's the attitude of borrowing more than just for education. What happens is, many are topping up credit debt because they need the best suit, the hottest car, the lush condo and what actually happens is, a habit is built that life is good spending money one doesn't have.

Far too many young people believe this to be the culture. What they don't realize, they have to eventually pay this all back. The right job comes along and if they're lucky enough to pay back debt at the bank and credit card company, they do it again.

They are adopting a habit that will keep them in poverty through life. Debt robs you of self-respect, and makes you almost despise yourself. Grunting and groaning and working for what you have eaten up or worn out, and now when you are called upon to pay up, you have nothing to show for your money; this is properly termed "working for a dead horse."

Simply stated, you are performing work for which payment has already been made, doing something, which is no longer profitable. Here's a story to show this allusion of the unfortunate sod that at some period bought a horse to work his field only to have the animal die before the field was ploughed and the animal still had to be paid for.

The same applies today. If you buy a car on credit, only to wreck it before the third payment is made, you are now working for a dead horse. I'm not referring to businesses or retailers buying and selling on credit, or of those who buy on credit in order to turn the purchase to a profit. Because borrowing to grow your net worth is a good practice after you do your due diligence. But I digress.

Another story is about an old Quaker who said to his farmer son, "John, never take out a loan; but if thee gets one for anything, let it be for 'manure, because that will help thee pay it back again."

Today that means save up a down payment for a home. Then borrow to buy the home because this will keep you busy and responsible. This advice may be safe to a limited extent, but getting in debt for what you eat and drink, wear and vacation is to be avoided.

Some families have a foolish habit of getting credit at "stores," and thus frequently purchase many things, which might have been dispensed with. Credit has to be paid back. And if you don't pay back the entire amount, interest rates chew up time and more money than any other feature of borrowing.

How many credit cards do you use? Or rather, use you? Count the ones from department stores, grocers and any in addition to the basic three, Visa, MasterCard and American Express, then imagine the interest rates you pay if they have unpaid levels against them.

Money is in some respects like fire; it is a very excellent servant but a terrible master. When you have it mastering you, when interest is constantly piling up against you, it will keep you down in the worst way.

But let money work for you, and you have the most devoted servant in the world.

It is no "eye-servant." There is nothing animate or inanimate that will work so faithfully as money when placed at interest, well secured. Eye-servant is a term used to work only when the employer is watching. Money works on your behalf night and day, and in wet or dry weather, whether you watch it or not. (more on accumulated interest later)

P.T. Barnum said, "I have discovered the philosopher's stone: pay as you go. This is, indeed, nearer to the philosopher's stone than any alchemist has ever yet arrived."

Does this sound like you? Be honest with yourself and really think about the answers to these questions.

- Do you have some months where money shows up just in time to pay the necessities, but you can't seem to maintain it for the long haul?
- Do you start out every month wondering where the clients and income are going to come from?
- Do you see other people making the kind of income that you want...but you have no idea how they're doing it?
- Has it been too long since you had the time and money for your family, yourself, or a great vacation?

The Art of Money Getting

- Do feel money or lack of money is your enemy instead of an asset?
- In short, do you feel like there's an invisible sinkhole draining your money and pulling you too down into it?

If any of those things sound familiar, I have some good news for you. None of those things are the real problem. Those things are just symptoms. The real problem is that you haven't changed your perceptions about some of these basic outlook triggers. (I'm going to explain to you what those are in just a moment.)

Once you change your perception and angle how you look at them . . .

1. You're going to have complete control over what you do with your money instead of money controlling you.

2. You're going to realize that invisible sinkhole draining you and your money was never even there to begin with.

Maybe things have gotten tough. Maybe you've gotten so burnt out in the day-to-day living, that it's just become a grind. And maybe you've lost touch with that initial spark of enthusiasm that you had.

You used to be excited to learn, to meet the love of your live, to move in together, to have a car, to fund a wedding, to have children. To play. To travel. To be happy. I'm going to show you how to get it back while you make more money and experience more freedom than you ever have before.

If there's one thing that I need you to know, that if you forget everything else you read in this book, **if** there's one critical thing you must remember, it's this:

There are your personal outlook triggers that keep you in bad habits. You want to change perspective, then hit debt hard between the eyes, knock it out, and allow money to grow for you. Look at what triggers you when it comes to money.

Now I'm going to walk you through exactly how to become aware of those triggers and make those shifts today to finally avoid debt once and for all. Oh, and by the way, since the old man who was looking for his son's piety was so damn rich, why didn't he just buy himself a bottle to suck? I didn't like that story, but it triggers a belief and ethics like no other. That's what money can be like. Ethical or not.

PHASES OF PROSPERITY

Hope you're excited and ready to get to know yourself a little better, finally tap into more courage, more zest for life, and more prosperity. I totally and irrevocably love a black bottom line. By the end of this book you will too. This section is a little workshoppy, meaning you will do a minute of looking a little deeper and answer a couple questions.

Now, don't be afraid or slam the book shut and toss it away. This is important because if you don't recognize yourself and your relationship with money, you won't attract much more. In fact, I'm going to tell you something very critical.

If you don't take your financial situation more seriously, you have bad taste in living a rich and full life and worse, you're going to suffocate and die a pauper's death.

I mentioned in my Preface that I discovered a pattern with my clients and I want to talk to you again about something that bothers them and maybe even you. You want the best for yourself because you strive to give your family a better chance at being happier. You want to be the best for your family and for yourself. It takes time, energy and especially money to be the hero expected of you, especially within the family framework today.

They have needs and wants. They expect and your dream is to provide. But what happens is, the wants overtake the needs and people get into serious debt. And yes, that sucks.

Kids especially know what's going on. Your friends know. Your family. You can't hide your frustrations, emotions and a being broke and in debt situation from them. You're only kidding yourself if you try. But it's not the end of the world. It's the beginning of a new adventure, the adventure of being your own and their best financial hero.

Are you game? You didn't find this book. It found you. It came to you because you are ready to make the commitment to live a better standard of life – and that means you want to know more and tackle how to reduce and erase your debt while increasing your income, am I right?

Know that even people in debt can be happier. If they plan things out and have a deep desire to make a change. I think you're ready to make that change. You can stop fretting and being angry with yourself right now.

Now let me ask you this, "What could motivate you to be happy and why would you want to improve your financial situation"?

A recent survey said that the most important aspects for a satisfactory lifestyle includes these:
1. Hope and motivation to having the freedom to do whatever you want.
2. To not care about what other people think.
3. To be emotionally and physically happy and available to your loved ones
4. To travel
5. To stay home
6. To be your own best ally

Now ask yourself this, "Are you willing to eat less and buy fewer clothes to save for the next dream trip or purchase?"

How about your dream to pay for a class, try a new hobby, spend time with friends, go camping – reflect on how to pay for that as opposed to just buying "stuff." How liberating would it feel when you could see a loan or credit card value reduce right in front of your eyes? Pretty awesome, isn't it?

Keeping up with the Joneses has a long-standing stigma about pushing and shoving to buy, buy, buy "stuff " just because your friends and neighbors have the "stuff". Frankly if you're not already aware, bigger and better and more has become a disease. Instant gratification has caused a lot of frustration, stress and oh yeah, debt.

But how did it get to this stage? Why have more and more people become obsessed with spending money they don't have? Because credit has made fools of us all.

Would you rather be in debt to the creditor for the rest of your life? Or would you rather live your dreams feeling calm by sorting out your financial situations and obligations?

The Art of Money Getting

Would you rather fight and claw to keep up with the Joneses? Or would you rather be the hero and example of being a smart financial cookie?

What would motivate you to stay away from bad debt and make good income increasing decisions? What is your heart's content? Would you like to know the first clue? It's simple. It takes courage and resolve to commit to become debt free. I believe you have the power and the strength to be your own hero. You can become a better example that your friends and neighbors would want to emulate as someone who understands personal relationships with money.

Personal finance is about setting yourself some life goals. Being frugal while you're young means you can have a wonderful life in your mid and later years. But if you're not young, you can still plan for the future. It's all up to you.

Here's something else about debt or in other words, the lack of enough income. You may be holding some of these more common negative feelings and frustrations.

- It's uncomfortable to think about.
- Sometimes you'd rather ignore it because you can be so hard on yourself.
- You feel overwhelmed even trying to think about money.
- All these uncomfortable feelings around your finances keep you frozen and feeling stuck.
- You may be saying to yourself right now that it's hard to look at your financial situation and you should be better off by now.

- You may still be thinking that things shouldn't be like this and you've wanted to change but sometimes it feels out of your control.
- It's easy to feel powerless when you think your finances shouldn't be like this.
- You're upset you got to this point.

All the ways that you judge yourself, remember that it's safe to give your feelings voice. All these emotions are already there but now you can give them a voice and let them go. As you address your feelings about money, remember these feelings no longer have control over you. Awareness brings change. It's safe to give your fears a voice and to finally let them go.

The other secret here is to put a different perspective on your current situation. We are about to do just that. I'll teach you several tools how to release the financial anxiety and overwhelm. You'll develop an easy to imagine energy shifting exercise using boxes, purses, wallets, conveyor belts, elevators and of course, a mountain.

- You can begin to let go of all these judgments that you have around your financial situation.
- Because even in your current financial situation, you feel calm and centered.
- Decide it's safe to let go of these feelings of overwhelm because you are in control.
- You are in control as you address your fears and take back your power.
- Deep down you know things are changing.
- Deep down you know you're capable of reducing debt and making money.

- When you come to that place of feeling better, you can begin to look at your financial position from a place of compassion.
- You're okay where you are right now because you know things are getting better.
- Going through this process any time you need to, you replace your overwhelm with the feeling of power.
- You choose to have patience.
- You know the power of the single step gets you more centered and clear.
- You only need to be clear on the next step.

One step at a time. At every step, you feel more powerful even though your current financial situation isn't the way you want it to be. But you are willing to take a step forward and focus on how it will become for you. Remember, when you feel better, more accepting of your situation, you will see new opportunities. You create better habits. You begin to let go of the negative emotions around money as you let go of the judgments and the comparisons.

You begin to see your own ability. Frankly, it was hard to see opportunity when you were overwhelmed but now you have the tools and actions steps in front of you to give yourself permission to be clear this is just the beginning.

- Make that commitment to reduce the intensity of the emotions around money when they come up.
- You will get clearer on the limiting stories you were told and have about money and you will begin to let them go.
- Make room for new beliefs.

- You can make money in a way that feels good.
- You have a lot of value to give.
- And today is a new day.

You will plant some powerful seeds when you're done this book. You will develop the skills of clarity and calm about your current financial situation because you are now more powerful than you thought. Today is a new beginning and you are ready.

Staying focused on uplifting emotions, taking a hard look at financial leaky holes, especially those in your mind, is a challenge you are supported and admired for taking. Fret, even be filled with angst and still, you will come out the other end busting a habit of putting yourself in debt, once and for all.

To be honest, even if you shift within a few days of reading, it takes as long as three weeks to have a new belief and emotional confidence to take root and stay grounded. So even though your debt may not disappear instantly, you will have the energy to tackle it in a way that gives you peace of mind and energy to implement a plan of action that will take you out of the red and into the black.

Let's look at the list below that outlines the 10 Phases of Prosperity and release of debt weight. After each item, rate how you feel about the concept on a scale of 0 (no emotional juice) to 10 (high intense, even uncomfortable feelings). Add up your score and this will be the marker you will work to lower throughout these next days as you read.

The bigger (higher) the score, the more you have resistance to playing out a life of prosperity. The bigger (higher) the score, the thicker your resistance to playing a better game of being debt-free.

The Art of Money Getting

You will soon discover (and probably feel badly about it) in most of the areas listed, more of your time and energy needs to be changed and refocused to clear mental thinking that debt is better than prosperity. That's right, you have a subconscious notion playing itself over and over right now, that debt serves you more than prosperity, otherwise you wouldn't be in this predicament.

How did this statement make you feel? Yes, this one you just read, "debt serves you more than prosperity"? Be totally honest with yourself here. Now, rate these top 10 phases of prosperity whether you agree, disagree, or willing to take action:

1. You believe in the power of your own ideas, dreams and thoughts. Isn't your capacity to create limitless and boundless? Aren't you big enough and powerful enough to find a solution to any financial challenge you face? Begin to believe again in your own ability to initiate solving your own financial challenge.
   0   −   10

2. Take complete inventory of your debts, write them down and come up with a GRAND TOTAL AMOUNT. By taking this step you will come away fully knowledgeable and aware of your present financial situation. Either you will be struck by the depth and gravity of your situation or you will be relieved by how little you owe.   0   −   10

3. Establish an easy functional workable budget that you can stick to and follow daily. You've

started to live a designed life, not an accidental one. You start living on purpose with your finances and you give up for good the "willy nilly happenstance". 0 – 10

4. Identify all your skills and abilities or giftedness, including the ones that you never use. Begin to view these as quick and easy steps to profits if you will only implement them. For example, I'm a writer and a coach. I've written copy for other people's websites and sales pages for the financial industry for years. In practicing this on myself I discovered that I've lost out on $50,000.00 during those first five years simply because I did not market myself as a copywriter or coach despite my training of 10 years. What a loss. What's your skill and gift? Do you acknowledge it? 0 – 10

5. Establish a structure for serving inside the area of your skills, abilities or giftedness. By becoming willing to serve, share and give, you position yourself to receive a reward equal to your service. Yet you serve for the sake of service and being a blessing, and let the income simply accommodate the service. You never get stressed out about money. 0 – 10

6. Understand and embrace the power of your personal oneness with your essence, higher self, providence, intuition (God) through your meditations and prayers. Don't underestimate the power of prayer. Know this from your

bones, that despite all your connection to spirit, nothing outside yourself can change your situation unless you take right action on what God provides. In fact, unless you "decide" you are worthy, put your low self esteem and low self confidence on hold, replace your belief about yourself, then only then, will you see the opportunities the universe provides for you. All the great wise and wealth gurus of the world comprehend this and live out this principle in their lives. (You will receive more information about energy and relaxation processes later.)   0 − 10

7. Tap into the notion that there is an Abundant Universe in control by giving away to a charity (tax deduction) or situation of your choice and what you feel comfortable with, financially and/or energetically of your time. This action frees you from the notion of scarcity and you enroll in the thought of abundance. You actually take on the posture and position within your thinking that there is more than enough to go around. You don't have to wait until you're a millionaire. You can share now. As a matter of principal, how about paying yourself first. Donate to your personal cause − you.   0 −   10

8. Tap into the belief in your own self worth by paying yourself first a tenth of your income. Why pay all your other debtors and not pay yourself? Aren't you worth something more than a few mere pennies? By paying yourself

first you start creating for yourself a new reality. It is a reality that will never allow you to say or think "I'm broke!" You may not have much but you'll never again be broke and over time what you have, will multiply. I keep a hundred-dollar bill in my possession at all times. I don't spend it, but if ever the thought pops in "I don't have any money", I am reminded I have lots even in the moment. I choose not to spend it right now! 0 – 10

9. Invest another ten percent in the "wheels of capitalism." Ten percent of your monthly income is enough for you to become an investor. (I invest 20%, but you decide how much for yourself.) Find a small business or utilize the one that you dreamed up or created through the implementation of your skills talents, abilities and areas of gift-ness and start creating wealth through your own personal investments. Now you're participating in the dream of your future. If you plan on investing in stocks and the market, I highly recommend you study blue chip only. Invest in those companies that pay you dividends. The rest are a gamble and a crapshoot. 0 – 10

10. Learn how to live on only 70% of your income. That's right. Scale down your life to fit within that box. Over time your income will increase and you that seventy percent will grow but in the present moment adjust your life and learn to live on seventy-percent. 0 – 10

What's your total emotional score? If it's more than fifty, you are courageous, honest and have a lot to shift. If it's below 50, you are courageous, honest and need a few more action steps to move forward. Be grateful you now know where you stand.

Did I scare you? I didn't think so. But remember what I said earlier, you're bound for the bag lady or street person if you believe that living a better structured financial lifestyle is for the birds. Because most people end up living off the government (which by the way pisses off tax payers) and barely scrape by.

GREMLIN PERSPECTIVE

Has that one person or a family culture in the previous chapter triggered emotions for you? Hope so because that's how to recognize the subconscious that replays and replays itself ruling your decisions.

It's critical to know yourself a little better, finally tap into more courage, more zest for life, and more prosperity. Notice if now you are reducing your score and moving yourself up the emotional scale. Are you feeling better even with this little bit of work about yourself? Because, here's what else happens. Once you become aware of those internal voices, your business and personal life will begin to prosper in new and profound ways.

That internal voice chatting back at you incessantly is a gremlin. Your business, your relationships, your finances cannot grow beyond your emotional response - nothing can grow beyond your emotional response. Everything matches your set point of emotions on every subject that exists.

Emotions are such huge factors when dealing with debt and your relationship with money. I really want you to recognize that this is the natural process you tend to use when thinking. A lot of your attention is on the hockey game, or the making dinner, or struggling with the kids, and not on the internal tape playing out how to feel especially about money.

That internal voice is not real. It's a recording of old programs that you heard and repeated often enough that it became part of you, automatically. It probably lies too. However, those programs do not have to leave you disempowered as a human being, because they were built on the notion that:

"I am not sufficient right now."

"I am not capable right now."

"I can't right now and there is something wrong with me right now."

"But one day when I get more 'stuff', or one day when I have the right circumstances then I will be enough!"

You can clearly see that bringing this attitude to your finances leaves you with a disempowered relationship between you and your money. You are not even aware of the fact that you live this way and think this way.

Believing that you are not enough now, leaves you living in fear now and carries forward onto the rest of your life unless you hear them. By feeling deficient now, it means that all you do is bring that perspective of brokenness and lack to yourself and to your finances. And here's the culprit to look out for, you beat yourself up because you think you're making dumb mistakes.

But it's not you. It's not a real you. It's what I call a gremlin belief. It's a stuck tape recorder from the past. How do you beat yourself up? From a financial management perspective, you go shopping and spending money you don't have.

As I think about it, I realize that I had made some mistakes in my life. I borrowed to buy myself a corvette in my twenties and didn't consider I couldn't drive it in our Canadian winters. Joke's on me.

I traded it in for a Camaro, which did get me through snow, but that debt was driving me bananas more than the glow of sitting behind the wheel of a hot car.

Stupid or stupid? Now I'm not saying don't take a loan out for a car or house or equipment you need. I'm saying, put it in perspective whether the make, model, size, cost is within your means. We'll come to means later in a later chapter.

Who else made a dumb mistake that cost you deeper debt you couldn't replay on a timely basis? All of us did something stupid, said something dumb, made a relationship-losing move, gave the wrong answer at the correct time, a correct answer at a wrong time - and so on.

Somewhere, sometime, somehow. We beat ourselves up and worse; someone who we thought loved us, beats up on us too. The solution is to become your own best friend. Easier said than done, you say? Well let me ask you this. If you don't clear away the anger, the guilt, the frustration, that memory is still there in your subconscious, haunting you.

It's as if you were carrying a backpack with all the rocks and boxes and bags stuffed heavy with the beliefs that don't work very well. Here's the good news. This is pure opportunity to grow and make yourself better.

Every mistake is a memory with emotion. If the emotion is positive, we can use that memory to create more of the same. If the memory is negatively charged, it repeats itself even if you don't understand why. You can learn from it and grow - but ONLY if you purge the dark energy surrounding the mistake. Today, remind yourself of the person(s) you saw reflected in your mirror yesterday.

It's time to set them and yourself free.

Remember that list of 10 from Chapter 1? Here's number 1 again.

1. You believe in the power of your own ideas, dreams and thoughts. Isn't your capacity to create limitless and boundless? Aren't you big enough and powerful enough to find a solution to any_financial challenge you face? Begin to believe again in your own ability to initiate solving your own financial challenges.

Read this next powerful exercise through and then try now to deal with a gremlin and begin to reprogram that subconscious mind tape player. First allow me to qualify that there is a myriad of ways to shift and clear energy. There are thousands of coaches and programs touting they can help you change. And there are thousands more who claim they can get you to "catch and release" a belief that no longer serves.

What I'm saying is it is impossible to release if you don't find the original source.

Our beliefs are our memories have found a groove in our internal record and keep playing over and over. Through the years of research and energy work, I have discovered and actually believe that once a negative belief, if discovered and brought to light, becomes 99% of the solution to dissolve it.

However, the one percent left, continues to run our lives despite our best efforts. And it's usually a murmur you decided as a child about money. Right or wrong, it replays until you tell yourself (your child) that's enough. Time for a new and better idea about money. Physics proves that energy cannot be created nor destroyed. So that energetic gremlin in the form of a belief can't be destroyed. This means the small percentage can run our lives.

Understanding however can shift it into something different. Here's why. Your awareness or consciousness focuses on what is happening either, here, now, or focus on your past or even the future.

When you decide something you just focused on is true and should work for you, your attention to it ingrains it into your unconscious, which now allows it to play and replay itself. From that point on, it works all by itself without your attention to it.

This has to be. It is natural because without the automatic, we couldn't possibly survive by having to consciously tell ourselves every time to do something. This then is the energy with which your life rides on. This now becomes a pattern, which plays out over and over. And because it originated from your thinking, it is energetically charged and it cannot be destroyed.

Now this new belief, takes on an energetic form, your original thought, which by the way is energy, is now an energetic replayed program. Yu decided that what you originally thought and believed, now plays out over and over, even if it creates negative results in your life. These are the ones you need to set free and change.

If energy cannot be destroyed, what the heck do you do with this now? You view it from a different perspective and literally send it to another dimension. You rethink of a new idea to replace it with and send the old to the dump.

Here's the exercise, which I know you will love. I call it "Gremlin Perspective".

Imagine you see and know which financial issue belief that doesn't serve you anymore. It could be "I'll never be rich." Or maybe it's a thought you borrowed from your parents, "Money is hard to keep." Whatever it is, imagine you can touch it, grab it and now put it into a large, heavy purse or wallet.

The purse is sitting beside you where you stand next to the mountain.

Once again, look at the negative pattern in the purse. Imagine how it looks and feels. Imagine its color and consistency. Just leave it in there.

Next, imagine you see elevator next to you, which will take you to the top of the mountain.

Leave the purse behind.

Once you reach the top of the mountain, step out of the elevator and look at the vista. Look way down at the purse at the base. You're okay. You won't fall even if you're afraid of heights. Look way down. It looks tiny or you may not even see it at all.

Knowing you can't make it go away, you know the issue is still in the purse somewhere below. Ask yourself how much effect has it on you now that it's so far away? How small is it? How big? Do you still want to carry the purse around with you?

Imagine you had on a harness that has hooks that you used to hold the purse on your back when your arms got tired. Take the harness off and drop it down the mountain. Let it fall away until it disappears along with the purse.

Now make a new choice about your finances. Decide now what you do want to believe that would act on your behalf that will serve you better. Turn away and walk back into your life.

You've just reprogrammed yourself. You're changed your perspective on an issue. Your intention and your mind have now caused a shift in perspective so that mentally and emotionally you feel differently about the purse of horrors.

Let me explain further.

1. The purse holds your old belief that is a pattern you could relate to. As long as it wasn't contained, it was difficult to separate yourself from the program. It ran you. You thought up to now you were the problem instead of the recurring pattern.

2. When you see the program as separate from you, the pattern has less power. And you carried it on your back all this time.

3. But now you have created a different perspective, one from a distance and now no longer feel trapped because it's outside of you.

4. Now that you made a new choice, you will act differently than from the previous ways.

5. When your focus was on the purse of issues, you couldn't see any other opportunities. Your vision was limited to the small space around the purse.

6. After riding up the mountain, you see a wider vista and experience a visual perspective much different than before. You see more opportunity and actions you could take.

7. Your subconscious responds with a new program, new ideas and a better feeling tape, freeing you to do things differently.

8. This simple imagining exercise reinforces the new change and widens your perspective so you can change your results.

9. And what about that purse with horrors in it? Ignore it. You can forget all about it. In fact, now focus on what you do want and keep your mind there. That makes the new energy bubble and grow.

10. You could now choose a different action step that will help you improve your financial situation.

This is all called quantum energy. It's shifting perspective. It's taking your power back, and most effectively, it's giving yourself a new positive approach to replay itself for the rest of your life.

You are no longer a victim of your circumstances because you are in control of how much energy you give a situation. You know how to change perspective with this unconventional method and can move easily into a conventional action step.

Great job today.

You did a lot of work today. Acknowledge and congratulate yourself for this commitment. You're on your way to erase the debt weight habit. Now instead of turning the page right now, I would encourage you to take a break.

Sit with your new perspective. Do something nice for yourself. Take a walk, a bath, drink of water, juice, sit in the sunshine.

When you've rewarded your work, come back and let's move on.

DEBT IS A DELICATE SUBJECT

There are probably quite a few more blobs, however, the one you discovered and left behind when you went up the mountain has the ignition key that triggers others.

You're probably thinking already about how challenging changing a habit can be, that is, if you believe it's difficult. The first thing I want you to do is to trust yourself and change your mind about the level of difficulty to change a habit. Tell yourself, "I can change my habits easily and effortlessly."

Second, energy is a scientific finding. Scientists like Albert Einstein have proved that energy exists beyond being a theory, but that we too are made up of energy. The mathematical equation $E=MC^2$ defines our mass, our bodies and ultimately, science also proves energy cannot be created nor destroyed. Instead, it shifts and changes and can be sent elsewhere.

Debt, the 4-letter word is a delicate subject for most people. People in debt do not want others to know their situations. And that's okay. I don't need to know your financial situation and neither should you worry that others in your life will know your situation that is unless you share it.

However, in order for the habit to dissipate and shift out, you must be absolutely honest with yourself. Telling yourself the truth of your debt is important because without knowing what you're dealing with, you can't make the change.

Remember those 10 Phases of Prosperity in Chapter 1? Let's look at the second one.

2. Take complete inventory of your debts**,** write them down and come up with a GRAND TOTAL AMOUNT. By taking this step you will come away fully knowledgeable and aware of your present financial situation. Either you will be struck by the depth and gravity of your situation or you will be relieved and enlivened by how little you owe.

I want you to do a little more than just writing down your debt estimate. I want you to discover your net worth.

Step 1: Add up your assets: These will include the value of your home, any retirement savings, savings account, black book value of your vehicles, and any tangible items like your TV, stamp collection and so on.

Step 2: Add up your debt: Take a deep breath and sit back and allow this to work itself out. Calculate the total you owe on your student loans, your credit cards, your mortgage, car loans, advances, amounts borrowed from family and friends, and any overdraft values.

Step 3: Subtract your total debt (from Step 2 above) from your assets (Step 1 above). This is your net worth, and the current picture of where you stand financially right now.

In other words, you know how much you own, how much you owe, and where you stand. Pat yourself on the back. You did a fine task to get here. Congratulate yourself for being willing to move forward.

If you have more debt than assets, what could you be doing now to help yourself out of this financial peril? Write down a few things you could be doing starting today. Don't be discouraged. Things will shift and you now have a few powerful tools to help you get into a better feeling state and put a different perspective on your situation. In fact, how about putting that net worth into a purse or wallet, drop it at your feet and take a ride up the elevator to the mountaintop? Go for it.

I don't want to leave you feeling bad about your situation. Your level of debt is actually irrelevant, because any amount reaps the same result: you come from a place of lack and are powerless. However, you need to know this value only as setting the bar NOT to exceed. Once you have this estimate, appreciate it because it is the opportunity to be dealt with. Become grateful because you created this. Yes, you.

You don't want to chastise and criticize yourself. You want to have integrity and begin a process you can be trusted. This by the way is the heart of the gremlin. Oh yes, it has a way of getting stuck as the truth as you experience right now.

But what's trust? I wrote earlier that a lot of people just don't have the trust in getting good advice about money. Trust is not from the outside.

Trust is all about keeping your agreements with yourself. Are you surprised? I'll do my best to explain from a quantum physics point of view. You see, when you break agreements with yourself, for example, you say you'll stop overspending and you don't stop but go ahead and spend again, you lose credibility with yourself. That loss of credibility radiates as energy from within.

EFFORTLESS BUDGETS

First, a heartfelt message for you. Great job so far. You understand that your purpose is to feel good about your life, financially and spiritually? Of course you do. That's why you're reading this book.

And you now know that you can help others as soon as you help yourself. You are very powerful. When you have an idea, have faith and clarity, the energetic field surrounding you connects with the overall universal energy and things align and manifest.

That's what Einstein and metaphysics experts define as the field. We live in an energetic field and what we think, we put into the field and it generated our experiences.

Anger, confusion, doubt, resistance, and resentment - yes, all these emotions could come up as you change debt habit. Up to now, you have aligned your energy, thoughts, and the field around you to manifest debt. You know it and I know it.

Today is a great day for you. With a newly reduced emotional rating from the top 10 Phases of Prosperity, you could now begin to balance your budget. Have I got you shaking in your boots?

Budget? Before I talk more about a budget, I want you to do one more little exercise for yourself. You have expenses that come up every month like clockwork. And if you pay them late, you get interest charged. So that bill grows bigger. On a piece of paper, list your monthly bills in order of due date and make sure you stay on top of them.

Now let's get back to your new challenge. Create a budget. Whether you know how to balance your bank statement, pay your bills on time, pay out your credit cards so you don't accumulate high interest rates, or whether you get nauseous at the pile of mail stacking up on the counter, the bottom line has been effected and the balance tells the story.

Creating a balanced budget has its benefits. The most important benefit is to prevent debt creeping into your life until it chokes you. Maybe you're already having trouble swallowing. Well, let's not lose another moment.

Even though this may bring you satisfaction or a sense of dread, the truth is that underneath you have a problem that needs to be addressed because debt can still accumulate if not previewed on a regular basis. As life unfolds, and as things become more and more expensive, it makes even greater sense you need to adjust to the flow of your money coming in and going out.

You need to learn to look at your financial situation way more often than you do. And when you do look at it, you must open your eyes at the reality instead of turning your back. Because what happens is, debt creeps up faster than you imagine. Debt creeps into the night, into your dreams, into your relationships, into your lifestyle, into your credit ratings and into your subconscious until it takes over your entire soul.

I'm going to make this as simple as possible. In fact, so simple, you may even have fun doing it. It's important to learn this one simple skill: balance your budget.

The government does it. Companies do it. Families with more money and less money than you have, do it. Ultimately, people with manageable to no debt have done it for decades and they reap the rewards in the end.

What's a balanced budget? Simply stated, it's managing to keep your income and expenses at about the same level. You may think it's too difficult to monitor. Rest assured, it will be challenging to begin with, but here's a quick lesson to get you started.

Go to that pile of bills and open them all. Add up how much you owe. Then look into your bank account and see if there is enough money right now to pay the bills today.

If there is, you can balance. If there isn't, please don't go into further debt, but instead, ask for help at the utilities companies or the bank to help you make some consolidation decisions to catch yourself up.

Normally, bills arrive once a month. Food shopping is probably more frequently. As any rate, estimate how much you spend each week and multiply by

4 to get a monthly food bill. Add some clothing allowance you absolutely require and now, this accumulated total will always arrive on time, every month. You need to know this total intimately.

Here's the next step. Write the total of your bills down on a big piece of paper and tack it up on the fridge, on a bulletin board, on your computer, in your smart phone, as a screen saver on your computer, at work, in your car, and tape it up on your bathroom mirror.

Now add some basic food costs, gas for travel (or other transit costs) because you have to get to and from your work. That is unless you are fortunate enough to work from home, so your expenses are slightly different.

Once you get your bank account up to the level you can pay these monthly, you are balanced. If there are any monies left over, of course, treat yourself.

And as you get better and better at balancing your budget, you may begin to have left over income that you can save and invest for your future. Eventually savings will be added to the monthly total and then you write that figure down and tape it where you can see it. Maybe it doesn't sound much of a budget strategy, however, if you don't begin, you will fall behind like over 80% of the general public. The debt ratio is outrageous and people struggle.

When people stumble, they get frustrated, upset and this low energy affects relationships and everything slides down. It's not the difficult. A pen, paper, calculator and a piece of tape. I'm sure you could find even more interesting ways to keep a balanced budget.

You can find electronic spreadsheets online almost anywhere. Type "budget spreadsheet" into Google or your search engine and see what pops up. Look for the zero cost and simple ones. Or just use sticky notes or flash cards. You only have so much money coming in. Be sure to list those expenses that you have to pay first, and make sure you don't overspend. Acknowledge and congratulate yourself for this commitment.

You might be struggling with really nailing how much you spend on your variable expenses. The bills you can list easily and they will probably be the same each month. But that pesky unknown that creeps out of the bank and you wonder what you have to show for it. Your variable expenses are things you can control. You'll be tracking them weekly from now on so you know what you're spending. Are you ready?

THE SOUND OF RESISTANCE

Say out loud, "I'm eager and willing to reduce and erase debt and have more money for the love of myself and my life."

If you're not there yet, maybe you are still stuck in some resistance that sounds like these:

"I have to do it."

"Fear is making me do this."

"My spouse/partner is making me."

"I've got to prove I'm a somebody!"

When you qualify your actions instead of feeling good and freely release the hold debt has on you, you continue to stay stuck, just enough that you won't see results. How else could you eliminate beliefs for good? I purposely decided to wait until well into the book to share more about the concept of energy, gremlins and quantum physics. Hopefully you planned a budget and are recording your expenses on a weekly basis.

So now let's chat more about the energy you are putting into these actions. I left the detailed chat about energy for now because, frankly, if I started spouting physics and fields and matrix phenomena in detail, you would close the book and read no further.

Plus, if you hadn't experienced some energy shift of perspective by now, you wouldn't believe me as much. So here goes. Back to school kids.

Remember in science class holding a magnet next to a batch of iron filings? The particles take a certain shape as they vibrate into a pattern around the magnet. The magnet shapes the filings because it has an invisible magnetic draw. A shield or field of magnetism surrounds the gravitational draw.

You already know your experience making a cell phone call or surfing the Internet without cables and wires. Yep. Same principle. These are also invisible fields for radio and TV. Well here's the clincher. Our minds and body have a similar energetic invisible field and by the power of your thoughts you are generating an invisible shaping field.

In other words, you are tuned in a certain vibration and you are the author of your own reality. Let me ask you this. Are you willing to stay being a victim of your parents or societies way of living? Are you staying a victim of your parent's financial situation? Or do want to believe you can make your life anyway you desire? Truthfully? It's up to you.

The field is the sole governing agency of the particle. Don't look at your situation. Look at your situation from the perspective of where and when you decided this situation was the only way to live. Your mind can change the level of wealth. It's the placebo effect. It means if you believe what your parent or advisor or spouse say is the definition of wealth, you will agree, follow and apply.

Your results will show you if it's a good definition or a stupid one. Even if you have positive thoughts about how to curb spending or invest and save money or live on a budget to stabilize your financial situation, it doesn't mean you will reach your financial goals without looking at the underlying habits playing and replaying themselves.

In fact, take a boo at the people who have won a lottery. Add a few million to their bank accounts and all hell breaks loose. They haven't conditioned themselves to the wealth. Stories surface that almost ninety-nine percent are broke in a couple of years.

There are mental breakdowns, suicides, murders, extreme poverty, divorce and outrageous debt after the fact. Read their stories. Heartbreaking because people forget or don't understand they need to clear out debt and un-wealth beliefs before bringing more money in. I don't want this to happen to you. The unconscious beliefs keep playing the original thinking even without you knowing.

Now aren't you glad you have this book? Let's get back to the principles. When you are having positive thoughts, you forget that you have the conscious mind and the subconscious mind. Both draw from the unconscious. One is automatic and the other, well it's up to you.

Your conscious kind is creative and works in the present moment. The subconscious is like a sub processor like in a computer and is a million times more powerful than the conscious mind. Your subconscious mind is running the show.

It has programs in it. The tape player isn't good or bad, it's the programs that are the source of limiting your abilities. Programs are those ingrained beliefs you have about life, your worth and wealth. If I have thoughts about making more money, I am pitting my thoughts against the subconscious processor, which operates, out of my belief system that could conceivably be what my 10 years self believes about money and how to make it.

And unless the subconscious is the same, as my dreams and conscious mind, only then will in get what I want. Otherwise I'm hooped and it won't happen no matter how hard I try. Besides, the subconscious is a million times more powerful. We need to look deeper.

What are you thinking? Doesn't matter. You can think about whatever you want because your subconscious mind is running your life. And here in is the rub. Without knowing your internal subconscious beliefs, which play out your wealth program, you will never change how things are. You will never reshape into prosperity for long periods of time. Worse is when life doesn't work or you don't get that wealth you want, you have a tendency to blame the outside for your lack.

The subconscious runs the show. And those tapes may not even be your own. They may be what grandma or dad or the president said about what you should believe about wealth. The other issue is you believe your own self-talk. Do you talk to yourself? I do. Most people think that if you talk to yourself, convince yourself of something, your underlying subconscious can change things. That's a myth.

Your subconscious is not another person. It's just a tape playing in a rut over and over. It's energy you created in the first place. It needs to be shifted and reshaped. It doesn't talk back nor reason with you. And remember don't be the victim of it. You are still in control as soon as you realize this.

So now that you know all the reasons you don't have more money and too much debt, what can you do about it? Look back into your first six years of your life. Your parents' behaviors are your behaviors. When you acquire these from other people you live out their lives and wonder why yours doesn't change. You've got to move on. How?

Attitude adjustment... yep... attitude. Attitude is simply a conscious choice that drives your physical learning and behaviors. I've said it several times now. Attitude is the most important factor in determining your financial success or failure. Attitude changes when you have enough information to make better judgment calls about your financial situation and understand what is happening with your money. Only then will your future security improve.

For example, you can choose to follow up on opportunities and you can choose not to. When you tell yourself not to follow up because:
- You don't want to seem pushy
- You're too busy
- It's too hard to get dressed and go out
- You're not sure what to say
- You're afraid of getting rejected

It's just your attitude that takes over.

In a study done by the Harvard Business School, results showed that top salespeople and producers:
- don't take "no" personally
- accept 100% responsibility for their results
- they don't blame the economy, competition, product
- they spend the bulk of their time on priorities
- they put themselves in their customers' shoes
- are self-disciplined and persistent
- are honest with themselves and the customer.

How many of the above elements could you relate to? Now it's time to examine your old notions and bring awareness to them.

Awareness may be all you need to dissolve an old pattern or belief. First, ask yourself, why would you want to heal old patterns that don't serve you? If you're struggling making basic ends meet, you might want to heal a pattern that keeps you from earning more or spending less. If you're constantly fighting with the very person you love, you might want to heal a pattern that keeps you from enjoying their company instead of going shopping because you feel entitled to heal your hurt feelings.

YOUR STRONG SKILLS

You're getting there. You may already experience calm and willingness to look at your debt as opportunities to shift into better relationships with your money and your intimate relationships. You may be wondering why it's taking so long to get to the meat and potatoes of the money management? If you don't bust through the core reasons you spend or don't save, no amount of earnings, budgeting, spreadsheets or investment opportunities will look appealing. You won't try them. You won't even see them.

By now you should have taken time to complete our budget and know how much money you're allowed to spend in each category. Again, categories are food, clothes, utilities, debt repayment, gifts, mortgage, rent, transportation, vacation, home renovations, education and so on.

Buy yourself a journal and take a page a week to write the amount you budgeted for each of the categories.

Food and personal care: $ budget/week
Transportation: $ budget/week
Entertainment: $ budget/week
Clothing and gifts: $ budget/week
Other: $ budget/week

Now keep track of all the items you purchased, date and dollar amount in each category. At the end of the week, total your budgeted weekly cash. Subtract the total you spent during the week.

Even though you feel better about taking action, there is still that time and patience required to have the old habit completely dissolve. Once that has dissipated, nature abhors a vacuum. You will need to replace the old with a new habit that supports you to reduce debt and increase income (savings).

4. Identify all your skills and abilities or giftedness, including the ones that you never use. Begin to view these as quick and easy steps to profits if you will only implement them. For example, I'm a writer

and a coach. I've written copy for other people's websites and sales pages for the financial industry for years. In practicing this on myself I discovered that I've lost out on $50,000.00 during those first five years simply because I did not market myself as a copywriter or coach despite my training of 20 years. What a loss. What's your skill and gift? Do you acknowledge it? 0 – 10

What are your strongest skills?

Do you really want to pay bills, make deposits, restructure your current expenses and begin saving a small percentage of your income? Are you looking for a new job? Can you create an effective resume to help you get the right job for you? Are you a single parent who feels challenged to take on more responsibility than you already have raising your children by yourself? Are you currently living pay cheque to pay cheque and can't see how you could make adjustments?

Would you rather work remotely and be available for your family? Can you get the job you say you want? Can you reduce the expenses you say you want to reduce?

90/10 RULES

First, let's recap the process. You must have a clear vision of what you want to accomplish and with whom. And it's not just "because" you desire something. Your vision must be so clear it feels as if it's real to you. You must have a support network in place you can consult with and mastermind with. But the caution here is that you must surround yourself with people who are at your level of support, love, confidence and growth.

If your best friend is deeper in debt than you are, don't ask his advice. If your sister has a nice nest egg saved, ask her how.

Interesting little story here. A client shared he was going to get marketing support from his friend to help him spread the word about his new business. But his friend was unemployed, in the middle of a divorce, drinking heavily and not such a good choice. You see, you need to be careful whom you surround yourself with. Energy is very important.

This brings us to this next bit. Find someone like a relevant mentor, coach or friend who will tell you the truth. Your mentor will tell you if you're on the right track and will gently (or not so gently if necessary) stop you from making the same mistakes. Don't get me wrong. Someone else doesn't know what will work best for you. However, sometimes looking at a decision or situation from the outside in with fresh eyes can reveal hidden clues to the next step.

Finally, you must be persistent and willing to go the full mile to reach success. That means a little ass kicking if necessary to take action.

What I discovered was that even if you followed all the criteria above, took action daily, were determined to make a success of your life, it could still fall apart in surprising ways that keep you dumbfounded. You keep wondering why it doesn't work. You see, what's missing here is the need for more clearing of that mental context (beliefs) you hold about yourself and other people.

What causes most distress is ignoring that inner critic that talks and talks and whimpers and cries at you day and night, "You can't do it, can ya? You're a loser. You'll never make it." You've given that voice the power over your life choices and now what? You believe the "stuff" of that little voice called a gremlin. However, it's not your fault. You picked it up most of it without evening knowing.

What are these dirty little secrets of programming in your mind and what can you do about them? Can you tell the difference right now if your mind chatter encourages you to step out and live bigger or does it squash and crash your dreams? Does it encourage you to take action or hide out in fear?

Become aware. Here's what to notice first. How you interact with people at home is how you interact everywhere else, including work. How you interact in personal relationships is how you interact in other relationships.

How you believe you are is how others perceive you. Ouch – now that came out of left field, didn't it? If you believe you're not worthy or not talented, or heaven forbid, not loved, people tend to pick up on that energy and respond appropriately. Then you say to yourself, see, I knew it, I'm a suck.

But let me tell you that it's the other way around. As soon as you shift your energy belief about yourself, you radiate differently and people respond differently. What else do I mean? For example, people may seem to shut you out without you or their knowing why. And that's because you believe you're not good enough to be included. You believe you are flawed in some way.

It took me a long time to figure out that when I thought I was protecting myself from people invalidating me, that energetic invisible shield kept people away from me. Even the ones I needed to help me grow and succeed. See what I mean? They act around you the way you expect them to from the inside out. The trouble comes when you do not know consciously you are doing this.

If you become aware of the way you think about yourself, you would become aware of why people treat you the way they do. That includes potential clients and lovers alike. Another example is if you hang around negative people who are doom and gloom sayers about economy and getting shafted instead of focusing on the successes, you stand a good chance of failing. Your energy becomes negative as well. If you're too occupied with planning, gathering, researching and more gathering, planning and researching, you stop yourself from doing what you originally wanted to do. Results don't come from just planning and gathering. They come from taking action to achieve the goals you set out. Are you taking action even if you don't really feel you're ready?

The trick is to become aware of what you are telling yourself about how soon you "should" get started. Then you can easily shift into action. That brings us to the game of the 90/10 Rule.

"Whew..." I hear you saying. "How's that even possible to be at the top of any game any time? What's this really about anyway?" Games in general all have rules. So does the game of life.

Here's a rule you may or may not be aware of. Either way, it's worth taking a deeper look into. The stories you told yourself every single day have lead up to this moment. And you either make up those stories or someone else told you things about you.

Here's the good news. More than 90% of the beliefs you operate out of and live by are someone else's. Less than 10% are your own.

Here's what I mean. A friend of mine who has been a follower of personal growth techniques for almost twenty years shared this to me the other day. She said she discovered a bunch of negative beliefs she had about completing a project that had a due date looming. We went through some of those beliefs.

"What if..."
"I hope I don't..."
"I should have said..."
"The client won't like me if..."
"I always have a problem with..."
"I probably won't finish anyway..."
"I can't believe how stupid I was to even try this..."

She then said, "I've been working on these beliefs for over 20 years. But something is still there. It's like the beliefs are sticky flypaper strips that won't move! So why don't those beliefs move out? The reason for the difficulty and longevity was because those were not hers in the first place. You can't budge, shift or change what's not yours.

You can only let them go and send them back to their original owners... parents, siblings, friends, bosses, whoever told you something about yourself that has plagued you most of your life. Here's what I want you to do next. Read this exercise through first, then come back and do it.

Find a comfortable chair in a quiet place. Sit upright with hands in your lap and feet on the floor.

Close your eyes, take a deep breath and as you exhale, imagine your whole body relaxing. And again, take a deep breath and relax. Keep your eyes closed and imagine that you know where the tension or blocked energy sits in your body.

Notice that it's stuck there. Breathe deeply again and imagine you are expanding your body to allow it to have more space. Pretend you are expanding space in your imagination until your body is as big as the room you sit in. Give that energy block as much space as it wants.

Good job. Now imagine that there is an energetic grounding cord connected from your tailbone down, down into the center of the earth. You could visualize a tree trunk running from your spine deep into the earth.

Imagine the energy block is now loose and ready to fall down the tree trunk away from you. Down, down, down and away.

Allow any thoughts or feelings that say, "This is stupid." Or "I don't believe it." Or "Ya, but, I can't just let her opinion slide away so easily!"

Allow those thoughts to flow down and away in the same way you gave that energetic block more space. Let those thoughts slide down the grounding cord or tree trunk. Gravity will draw them away from you.

If more blocks show up from other people in your life, allow those to slide down. Keep doing this until you feel complete.

Oh, one more thing.... Some things of high-value aren't always easy to reach.

Good health, quality relationships, and a profitable and enjoyable business – all take time & effort to create and maintain. But before you dig into more debt to hire a coach, or buy the next best promise, take stock of why you want these things that you think may make your life better.

Are they what you want or what you heard someone else has been telling you?

And keep that weekly journal of what you spend. I trust you that you keep track of your expenses. A holiday weekend like Thanksgiving can put a dent into your bank account. A turkey, side dishes, dessert. They all cost. Write it down.

13 BEST MONEY SAVING PRACTICES

Here now are the top 13 of the fastest and most effective ways to get out of debt, pay down debt, and feel 100% better about yourself.

You may not realize this, however, the percentages of people carrying debt is proportional and comparable to the percentage of people with health issues. Does that surprise you? It shouldn't because if one is feeling crappy and frustrated about money, one is feeling crappy and frustrated about life in general which, in turn, affects your mind and your health.

Health and wealth are tied closely. People are waiting to get a disease according to the medical researchers. The current emotional, environmental, and cultural constructs tell us we will get diabetes, dementia, depression, oh dear, so many diseases... and people are buying into how easy it is to be sick.

You've heard and seen the ads, "1 in 4" will get cancer. Well, the same principles apply to finance. Beliefs and self-imposed limits get people in trouble and most don't even know why.

But now, you know to check inside, to check what you're telling yourself, and now you know a tool or two to self heal. You have taken huge strides to become more responsible and feel better about your situation.

If you're ready to pay down your debt or get rid of it altogether, here are the top lucky 13 general suggestions. Besides growing a healthier bank account, you will find your own energy and spunk levels increasing. There really isn't any one "best way" that works perfectly for everyone. Take what will work for your situation and ask the experts to help you more.

1. Pay More Than the Minimum

An obvious credit card and loan principle, more often gets ignored. Even the lenders don't want you to pay more because they want to get more interest from you. Even if you added an extra $10 to the minimum payment, you are giving yourself a better chance to pay down faster. You can find 6 different payment calculators here: (cut and paste this link into your browser)

http://www.nomoredebts.org/learning_credit/calc.html

2. Spend Less Than You Plan to Spend

I mentioned in a previous chapter that I was going to speak more about living within your means. This is one of the most important aspects to get into the habit of doing.

For example, you "need" a new pair of shoes for work vs. you "want" another pair of shoes ... just because. My parents taught me that "You can have al-

The Art of Money Getting

most anything you want; you just can't afford everything you want."

Many people get into debt and stay in debt because they tend to buy what they want, when they want. Not even millionaires can afford to buy everything they want. If you want something, don't buy it unless you have the money. The long-term consequences are worse than the short-term satisfaction.

Instead, learn to be satisfied with less than you would ideally want, even temporarily, so you can use the money you save to pay down your debt first. By the time your debt is paid off, you'll probably have adjusted to your new priorities, and you can use the money that you are saving to put towards other financial priorities. And then, only then, consider the toy. This is a big lesson, but an important one to really take seriously.

3. Pay Off Most Expensive Debts First

A lot of people have more than one credit card, a mortgage, a car loan, and a student loan and maybe even more. It can be overwhelming. Here's one of the smartest strategies for getting out of debt even if you are overwhelmed.

Make minimum payments on all of your debts and credit cards except for one. Choose the one debt that is charging you the most interest and focus all of your extra payments on paying that one off first. It's important to note that you should never add to this one that you are currently diligently paying off.

Because, once your first, most expensive debt is paid off, take all of that money that you were paying on that first debt and focus it on the next most expensive debt. Continue this method as you pay down each of your debts, and you will be left with your least expensive debt to pay down last. (Which you all the while are still paying minimum payments).

This strategy will get you out of debt quickly, and you will feel encouraged as you see your progress. How quickly is relative, however, it will surprise you that paying off the principle AND the interest is impressive when you see the value reducing and reducing.

4. Buy a Quality Used Car Rather than a New One

We used to buy a new truck every 6 years or so. They cost about $40,000 to $50,000 and we never paid off the loan from the one to the next. That meant we were in perpetual debt.

Then I read Dave Ramsey, a personal finance radio host, who once said that, "A new $28,000 car will lose about $17,000 of value in the first four years you own it. To get the same result, you could toss a $100 bill out the car window once a week."

Since understanding how new vehicles lose their value driving off the lot, we now look at 1 to 2-year-old vehicles. They cost less than half and are in perfect condition. You can save yourself thousands of dollars if you buy a quality used car rather than a new one. The money you save can help you get out of debt much faster. Once you have zero debt, money piled up in your bank account, sure, go ahead and buy yourself a new car.

5. Consider Becoming a One-Car Household

If your family has two or more cars, consider getting rid of one and either walking to work, taking transit or car-pooling. Now I'm not advocating this for everyone, however, if you are in dire debt, they may save you years of paying down. You can save yourself thousands of dollars a year by using one car.

If you use this money to pay down your debt, it will make a big difference. Instead of going cold turkey and selling your second car right away, test-drive this idea first. Try parking your car for a while, dropping the insurance down to pleasure use only and see if taking transit, walking, cycling or car pooling works for you. If you do decide to sell your second car, even the odd taxi trip or rental car won't amount to nearly as much as you would spend on keeping your second vehicle permanently.

6. Save on Groceries

Here are some household budget tricks to save money.

http://www.mymoneycoach.ca/money_management.html

Things like, stocking up on groceries when they are on sale, or stockpile when they are on sale and then skip one grocery shop every month and live off of the food you stockpiled are a couple ideas you could consider. You can stockpile non-perishable groceries like canned goods, cereal and things that you can freeze like bread and meat. Filling your cupboards when groceries are on sale and then skipping one grocery shop each month can save you up to 25% on your annual grocery bill. A family of four could save $2,300 to $2,900 a year by doing this. Applying these kinds of savings to your debts will definitely put you ahead in the long run.

When you "skip" a grocery shop you will still need to buy perishable groceries like milk, fruit and vegetables, but hopefully you can skip the rest of what you would normally buy. If you can't skip a shop once a month, then try for once every other month. That will still save you a good amount of money.

7. Get a Second Job and Pay Down Your Debt Aggressively

Getting a second job, or consistently picking up an extra shift or two, is a common way for many people to pay down their debt. This doesn't work for everyone, but if you can make it work, you could be debt free within a short number of years.

One of things we did in our household was using my income to pay down all the debt and living off my husband's. We learned to manage our lifestyle to accommodate the available income. It worked because we were able to reduce and erase our debts in a few years. Once the debt was gone, we continued this lifestyle and added my income into savings and investments.

For this to work for you, you may need to apply all of your extra income to debt repayment. Working the extra shifts or hours also doesn't need to be permanent. Once your debts are paid off, you can look at scaling back again.

8. Track Your Spending and Identify Areas to Cut Back

For some people, doing this can save them almost as much money as working a part time job. You won't know how much you can save unless you give this a try.

It's called track and see. Earlier in a chapter I asked you to look at which expenses are more prevalent and which are unnecessary. Now you want to actually keep track of where you spend your money because it will surprise you because most of us spend unconsciously and get surprised at the end of the month about where the money went.

Here are more tools to track expenses.

http://www.nomoredebts.org/learning_credit/monthly-expense-tracker.html

Tracking will show you what you are spending not what you think you are spending. Try it over the course of a month. If you aren't honest with yourself in this exercise, it won't work. Once you know your spending habits, you should be able to identify areas where you can cut back. Allocate the money you "find" to paying down your debts.

9. Get a Consolidation Loan

Take advantage of your bank or credit union. You tell them what you want. They can help you consolidate all of your consumer debts into one loan with one payment at a lower interest rate. This can be a helpful first step in getting your debt paid off.

However, getting debt consolidation loan will only help you if you create a budget that allows you to save some money every month.

Savings isn't usually what someone in debt thinks of first, but if you don't have savings, you will likely need to reapply for credit cards part way through your loan and then rack up more debt. The end result could leave you worse off than before. Here are a few more tips where to find consolidation support.

Here's a Canadian resource.

http://www.nomoredebts.org/debt-help/debt-consolidation.html

If you are from the U.S. or other countries, go directly to your bank today.

10. Refinance Your Mortgage

In the wake and thick dust of the subprime mortgage fiasco of a few years ago, if anything, that should open your eyes to becoming informed and understanding the fine print.

However, what most people don't know is that accepting the mortgage payments and structure offered is not supporting you to pay down your home on a timely and supportive basis. That is, if you own your own home. You may have enough equity to consolidate all of your debts into your mortgage.

If you don't have much equity in your home, additional mortgage insurance costs may be expensive. Make sure you consider all of your options and seek advice from someone other than your lender (since they have a vested interest in getting you to choose this option). Just like with a debt consolidation loan, when you consolidate debts into your mortgage you also need to create a budget that allocates money to savings. If you don't, you'll always be tempted to borrow more when "emergencies" arise.

Repeatedly using your home as an ATM can set you up to face retirement with a lot of debt, no assets and no savings. Terrible way to live out your "golden" years.

11. Speak with a Credit Counselor

If you are in debt and think that bankruptcy might be your only solution, start by speaking with a credit counselor. Find out what programs are available to help you deal with your debts. A reputable Credit Counselor will explain all of your options and let you choose the option that makes the most sense for you in your situation.

Many people don't know what they need to know about debt repayment programs at non-profit credit counseling organizations but most are relieved they took the time to find out before it was too late. Speaking with a non-profit Credit Counselor about your options is free, confidential and non-judgmental. Search for one in your local area.

http://www.nomoredebts.org/debt-help/debt-repayment-and-bankruptcysolutions.html

12. Create a Spending Plan

Another name for this is budget. A budget is just that - a spending plan. And I wanted you to start one by now. It will help you stay on the straight and narrow with your current debt payments, or your new accelerated payments.

A spending plan is something you lay out to make sure that you are spending less than you earn. Some people say that they don't like budgets, but have these people ever tried one? Better yet, if you've lived all this time without a budget, how do you know you won't like having one? After trying a realistic budget on for size, most people agree that the alternative--being in debt--is much worse.

Lucky 13. Pay yourself First

Did you know this is the greatest of all money saving tips?

Pay Yourself First.

I didn't say spend on you.

I said pay you.

This is a very, very important key to building wealth in your life. If you understand the concept and fully absorb it, it will virtually change the way you feel and act towards money and your current financial situation.

- It doesn't matter what your current situation
- It doesn't matter how much money you are making or how much debt you have
- It doesn't matter.

You need to pay yourself first.

By paying yourself first, you are actually creating a new "mindset". Going from a mindset of:
- "I am broke"
- "I don't have any money" to …
- "I do have money"
- "I am not broke"
- "I can save"
- "I can build wealth"
- "I have the power to change my life"
- "and yes, I can be wealthy"

This one little action will literally take you from that old, broken mindset to a new freeing, empowering mindset. Don't live in that broke mentality anymore! Nope, don't do it. You will be going from a point of having a "poor mentality" to having a "rich mentality". Yes, think rich.

Don't wait until you are making $100,000 or $500,000 a month to think rich. Think rich now. Here's another easy way to shift thinking.

Go into a worry, fear or doubt. Interrupt it with a pleasant memory like someone you love or an experience that was joyous. Your brain can only hold one idea at a time. The worry or the pleasant. You can control and reshape your brain by using the pleasurable memory overlapping the worry.

Pick a word that can trigger this. Use a word like love, or peace or joy or peanut butter. Just kidding. Or maybe peanut butter is a joyous trigger word. You find a word that fills you with kindness and power.

Fill your mind with this instead of the doubt and fear. Now tell yourself, "pay myself first". Allow it to fill you with good feelings. Because when you do this, you will have money. You will not be broke.

My word(s) are Zane Grey. I read his little cowboy stories ever since I could read. And I felt safe, excited and in charge of my own life – even at 8 years old.

Where do you pay yourself first? Into your savings account. Into an RRSP. Into an investment that will grow exponentially. You will not have to live pay cheque to pay cheque. Do you see it now? Do you see by paying yourself first, you are indeed building wealth in your life?

You have to pay yourself first to get out of the mentality of "thinking like a poor person." You will be getting out of the conversations of:

- "if I only could save some money each month"
- "if I only could have money"
- "if I only could

By paying yourself first, you will think rich and then you will grow rich. Think above and beyond your current way of "Being".

Rich Dad Poor Dad says: "Rich people are Bigger than their problems. Poor People are smaller than their problems." What does that mean to you? Rich people already think on a big scale.

- they think abundantly
- they not only think they are larger than their problems
- they KNOW they are larger than their problems.

- Poor people think about their problems:
- they dwell in their problems
- they stew in their problems
- they let their problems consume them
- and guess, what? They love them!

Start off with just 10% of your income. Put it away. Save it. You deserve it. You deserve it. What are you working for then? What are you working for if you are not rewarding yourself? If you are the one working shouldn't you be the first one to get paid?

(Please say yes).

Is that what it means to pay yourself first? Yes, set aside at least 10% of your income for you. Put it in a separate account. We can call it your LOVE ME account.

This will take you out of the poverty mentality. You will begin to feel different. You will begin to act different. You will begin to relate to your financial world with more power. And, you will begin to relate to your money and finances differently.

DEFINITION OF WEALTH

Now let's churn things up, shift sideways and look at the debt situation from a different angle. Could you honestly say to yourself or out loud, "I appreciate and feel wealthy in my current financial situation."

Yes? No? Let's talk about it.

Most people recognize the concept of gratitude. I would like to take this concept a step further and even though you may think it's just semantics, I'd like you to grab a dictionary and define the word gratitude. Found it? Now look up appreciation.

Not much difference is there?

However, from a financial perspective, there is a huge difference. You see, appreciation is a term used in finance to define growth. Gratitude is not about growth, but about feeling good in the present moment.

Think about it. What is it you want? To reduce and eliminate debt and to increase and maintain profitability, right? In order to do so, you must get your mind, body, spirit and all the energy around you synced to "appreciate" which signals everything from gratitude TO grow.

Next, let's define wealth and the state of feeling wealthy. If you don't feel wealthy now, how can the universal forces, energy, providence and yourself send you things that produce that feeling of wealth to you?

If you don't define how wealth feels, you will not experience it even if you are wealthy. Maybe you're already wealthy but you're talking yourself out of it because you don't know how it should feel for you?

Grab that dictionary again. What does it say about wealth? It defines it with all the terms we are familiar with: fortune, abundance, prosperity, luxury, money, opulence, riches, and affluence. But how does it feel to be wealthy? This is your task - imagine that scenario in the mirror. Redefine how you would feel in your state of wealth. How does it feel? What emotions come into play?

In a recent interview, Christianne Northrup, MD said that one of her coaches healed a sore throat within moments. What he did was remind himself "Even though I have a soar threat, I appreciate it because it has something to tell me. I appreciate and love it for being part of me."

Dr. Northrup said that when we appreciate where we are, whether physically, emotionally, spiritually, we are automatically opening up to receiving healing and greatness.

This so works for money. Now come back to the affirmation:

"I appreciate and feel wealthy in my current financial situation."

You've opened up to possibilities. Watch for miracles. They will show up as you move forward taking even the tiniest action to reduce and erase the debt weight!

What else will you do today as an action step to increase your appreciation of your wealth?

HOW TO HAVE IT ALL

Hey... remember those phases of prosperity? How did you score on #7 of the **10 Phases of Prosperity?**

7. Tap into the notion that there is an Abundant Universe in control by giving away to a charity (tax deduction) or situation of your choice and what you feel comfortable with, financially and /or energetically of your time. This action frees you from the notion of scarcity and you enroll in the thought of abundance. You actually take on the posture and position within your thinking that there is more than enough to go around. You don't have to wait until you're a millionaire. You can share now. As a matter

The Art of Money Getting

of fact, why not pay yourself first? Be your own charity. Pay you.
0 – 10

Today's challenge is to really look at your relationship with whom and what you believe supports you. Today I want you to make another shift in your belief system about money. Why not create a thinking system so powerful your money talks back at you?

People don't like to talk about their debt. Guess what? People don't like to talk about money period! Has it ever occurred to you that your supply of money could become an endless possibility? A supply of endless possibility . . .

Are you one of those people that live in the world of "I don't make enough", or . . . "If I only made $1,000 more a month . . . how different life would be"? You were asked in the last section to look closely at some beliefs about money. Now, ask yourself whether you operate in the context that your money supply is limited or outside your control? Well, in this challenge, I want you to address this notion. So, if you think your money supply is limited, you're about to change your mind for good.

Your money supply is not limited.

And guess what else? You have control over your own money supply.

Did I just hear you gulp? Listen, whatever it is that has you stuck, whatever it is, that has you stopped, might not even be about the amount of money you're making or the amount of money you're spending.

What might have you stuck is your own belief that something or someone outside you is controlling

your supply of money and inside that belief, you will forever remain stuck because . . .
- you have no relatedness to your power and
- no relatedness to your ability
- you don't know what is possible.

And, through the exercise of your own personal power, you can harness your ability to develop and maximize your own money supply.

Have I got you confused? Let me repeat this. You can harness your ability to develop and maximize your own money supply.

Let's look closely; you'll see that your money supply can be increased in many, many different avenues; you begin to see a different approach to control. First, let us explore the common avenue of wages.

What are wages?

It is income earned through employment. But, how can you increase this money supply?

You could work an extra shift.

You could get a part-time job.

You could make it a family affair and have your son or daughter pick up a newspaper route or get an after-school job.

You could ask your boss for a raise. When was the last time you asked?

When you have conversations with your boss, remember, have conversations that are big.

What do I mean by big? Have conversations that will enlarge your territory, add more responsibility, and conversations that leave you with a bigger money supply.

Money supply and increasing it, is an Empowering initiative for you to take on.

The Art of Money Getting

When you make money supply a family affair, you will be surprised how much they want to help.

You could enroll your son, your daughter, your wife, and your husband in examining this question: How can we, as a family, take on increasing our supply of money?

These are new ways of thinking, acting and being that will result in more money supply. Where we have all failed in this concept, is a result of our inability to recognize that supply is not fixed, nor limited. New supplies of money can be created.

Having said that, the concept is not to bring "down" your family into thinking lack. The concept is to bring "up" the energy and notion it's fun to earn and save. They will have ideas you may never have thought of. Be open minded. AND positive!

But first, you must recognize your power to create.

By recognizing your power to create your own supply, you will begin to exercise a new ability in the way of your own personal humanity.

This new ability or this new recognition gives you access to new ways of thinking.

You will re-invent yourself as a possibility of generating as much supply as you want. This could be a new thought pattern – that money is unlimited and that you just have not tapped into the source for how much you need and want.

Before thinking this way, you never would have thought of what else could be done to make extra money. So, now that you know that your money supply is not limited, you can actually begin to create new ways of generating more money for yourself. Money generation is in your power.

Please don't get underwhelmed that a paper route is more money. It certainly is. And for the right aged child (or yourself) it can be a source of exercise, enjoyment and entrepreneurship like no other. Let them do it. Because now your family has that extra cash to pay for an arts program or sports program for your child.

Underwhelm is a bad habit just as debt is a bad habit. Underwhelm will sabotage your efforts. If anything, begin to feel appreciation for even the smallest increase because again, providence moves to support you having more when the energy lines up and shows your intentions.

Here are the steps I want you to take in today's challenge. Your first step is to list what aspects of your money supply you believe you can control. For instance, list your income earned through wages.

Now list any income that can be achieved through other avenues. Begin identifying creative opportunities for increasing your money supply. For example, car-pool to work and charge a fee. Brain dump. Jot down any and all ideas that flow through. Don't judge, write.

What skills or abilities have you not implemented because you feel you're not good at them, or you feel you're not adequate in that skilled area? What would happen if you were to take a few moments a day and work at that skill until you perfected it and then you were able to expand and maximize your money supply by implementing a new and exciting skill that you have never used?

For example, what would happen if a nurse were to go and get specialized training in a certain area like flu shots at the local pharmacy or school? Now for

The Art of Money Getting

the same amount of time and money, or time and effort worked, that nurse will earn more money because that job will pay more.

So, instead of looking at your current money supply, look to see what hidden talents or skills you possess right now, those you have not been using, and with which, if you were to use, would naturally net you more money.

The second step is to tap into your intuition, or higher self (intuition) and trust that that connection will bring you more ideas that are just right for you. I call my inner connection providence. It (she) (he) supports me and moves in the directions I want to have manifest in my life when I make the commitment. Believe that when you are relaxed and asking the right questions, miraculously, answers come to you.

The third step is all about wild ideas. You know that ideas are abundant, don't you? You could come up with the most outrageous, or common-sense ideas at a drop of a hat, couldn't you? Begin to just write wild ideas about what's possible in the area of your money supply. For instance, list income you can create. Let your mind freewheel through what is possible for you in creating additional income by beginning to examine in what way you could increase your money supply by accessing those creative aspects you may have previously ignored.

Stop poo-pooing outrageous ones. List them. You'll be surprised how much you can come up with. And finally, take that list, pull out an idea that resonates best for you and make a commitment to begin implementing it. Go for it. You have nothing to lose and everything to gain.

What does it take to save a million dollars? Well, a million may be too huge if you are in debt and can't fathom that stretch. Let's look at a little or a lot, depending on when you start.

A 30-year-old who contributes $3,000 per year to an RRSP, earns an average of 9% per year for 35 years has $705,373 at 65.

If you started saving at age 25 same investments, you will have $1.1 million age 65.

Easy. Right? If only you'd known back then what you know now. Like Rod Stewart sings, "I wish I knew what I know now, when I was younger."

Let's look at this in reverse. If your goal is to have $1 million by age 60, how much do you need to invest? Pick a reasonable rate of return - 13% per year is reasonable in a good-performing mutual fund) Now how many years are you before you reach 60?

- At 25 you require $118 a month
- At 30, $225 a month
- At 35, $445
- At 40, $882
- At 45, $1820 a month.

Looking at this another way:

$500 per month, earning 13% at 55 and retire at 60 gives you $42,000:
- At 50, $122,000
- At 45, $275,000
- At 40, $567,000
- At 35, $1,235,000
- At 30, $2,186,000
- At 25, $4,250,000

Surprised? A $1,000 per year RRSP Beginning at age 25 will accumulate more by the time you're 60 than $3,000 invested every year beginning at 40. It's not the rate, it's the time. And it's compound interest.

Get yourself in an investment program. Note: don't go to the bank or trust company. They look after themselves. An independent financial planner is the better alternative.

ESTABLISH A TIMELINE TO REACH YOUR GOALS

This next section will guide you to solidify your intention to release the habit of debt. So far, you were looking at some of the beliefs and voices in your head that kept taking you in a greater debt direction. You want a shift to take place and hold you grounded with expectation and excitement for at least the next couple of weeks so you feel it worked and becomes permanent. How can this occur simply and effortlessly? You have already established your intentions to pay down debts and increase savings.

The next step often puts people off. Eyes roll skyward and you can hear the huff ever so slightly come out their lips. Don't huff.

The answer is set goals.

Goals?

Yes, goals.

Goals are important to your over well being and financial plan. Have you started to implement your plan? (Please say yes). Please say yes you have opened a bank account and are paying yourself first. Goal one done.

Your financial plan is also made up of a series of other goals that you will achieve. Let's clarify the definition of a goal. A goal has three major components:
- it is specific
- it is measurable
- and it is time-bound

Let me give you an example.

A goal is something you have a deep desire to attain. It has a purpose and an objective and it is something you are striving for. It can be quantified and time specific. For example, "I want to save $5,000 over the next six months starting a month from now." This example has a desired outcome and it is also time specific.

Your turn. Understand that your entire financial plan has to be time bound and specific. Establish your financial plan with a timeline for achieving results because money grows - over time.

Your financial plan should look like a list of specific measurable objectives to be achieved, one right after the other. As well, your entire financial plan has to have a defined timeline for every goal in that plan. Are you ready? Are you ready to make you list and implement it? If you find yourself self-talking or thinking along the lines of "I was going to do this."

Or "I was going to do that."

Or "I don't want to do that".

Remember all those promises we make to ourselves?

You remember those New Year's resolutions over the years that you have declared that you would do? Have you? It's never too late to begin. How many of those promises and goals have you been able to bring into existence? Did they fall by the wayside be-

The Art of Money Getting

cause you did not set a goal or have a plan? Wishful thinking is just that wishful.

However, when you put it into action with a plan, time tested, you will see results. I promise you that if you look closely, you will notice that any goal you accomplished was the one that had a timeline you promised to accomplish. And you did. Therefore, one of the key elements to success and making goal setting powerful is to create and design your life around the outcomes you want to achieve in your life. Again, goals are specific, measurable, and time bound. But there's another element. It has to be SMART.

S - specific
M - measurable
A - attainable
R - realistic
T - time bound

And because it's made of your goals, let's declare that your financial plan is S.M.A.R.T. Making your financial plan S.M.A.R.T means establishing a timeline. You must be able to measure it to see how effective it is. Otherwise, change it. Not having an established timeline for following through with your financial plan just won't give you:

- results in your life
- a powerful life, where your word becomes action thereby causing results
- a fulfilled life

Now, can you see that you must have a plan in order get yourself out of debt and start building wealth? There is a light at the end of the tunnel. Do you see it? Declare everything you want in your life. Declare to yourself you are the possibility of having anything you want in life knowing that your plan for achieving this is solely determined by you. It is in your power. Make your goals powerful. And, make your financial plan powerful as well.

Just know that you have much power and know that you can set goals all day long but if you are not setting SMART goals, then they then are of no use. They won't motivate you, they won't drive you to move forward and they won't take you out of your comfort zone. You just simply will not achieve, accomplish, or get the results you are trying to get. Instead, you will be left frustrated, upset, and still broke and in debt.

If you are not willing to do these things, then goal setting is just an exercise in futility and a complete waste of time and you will continue to live in a wish, a hope or a dream. Recognize that what it takes to accomplish the goal is ultimately you redesigning your way of "being" and your "life".

Take on being in a way that you have not been before. Here's the other reason your plan has to have impact on you.

You generate a vibrational energy when you feel good about something. This vibration sends signals to others around you that you are on a mission. Just as you're feeling bad about yourself or neutral doesn't send a vibration and isn't picked up, not feeling happy doesn't generate any action.

This brings me to the purpose of your goal. The purpose of your goal is to discover or to confront "who you have to be" in order to reach that goal. Who do you have to be? How do you have to redesign yourself? How do you have to act and think in the "face of" being different? How do you have to be is to become completely different from before. Only then will you have a better chance to reach a goal that you have set for yourself. How do you have to be? How do you have to become? You will have to be totally unlike the way you are now in order to achieve your financial plan in your established timeline.

You have to change. Until now, you have probably related to your goals as if they are reality. Goals are not reality. What you are seeking in your goal does not currently exist. Goals are a possibility, a guide and need to be accepted as a possibility into reality.

What stands between you and your goals is the same thing that is standing between your possibility and your reality. Right now, your goal is your possibility of what might happen, what could happen, what's possible. Think about it. What stands in the way between your current reality and your future possibility?

You.

Maybe there is something between you and the results you say you want? I'm being totally frank when I say, there is one thing that stands between you and your dream.

Action.

You need to take action to turn your possibility (goals) into reality. Therefore, action is the missing link between your goals, what you want to accomplish, what you hope to accomplish, what you wish to accomplish, what you dream of accomplishing, and the reality of what you are sitting right in the middle of. If you don't take action, then you will continue to experience what you have right now. And, is that what you want? (Please Say No). In this section, I am offering a couple of steps that I want you to take action to implement in your life right now.

One more thing, it's not enough to take action unless you feel good about it. If you're huffing and puffing and grimacing while stomping your feet you don't want to act on making a change, remember this, nothing good ever came from doing something with a scowl, attitude and damning the process.

All you're doing is staying stuck. Action should be accompanied with a feeling of appreciation, gratitude and hey, go ahead, put a little grin on your face. The first step is to declare a timeframe for achieving your tangible (e.g. buying a house) or intangible (e.g. getting out of debt by reducing an 18% interest generating credit card which will never get paid off if you apply only the minimum amount!) desired financial outcome. In fact, let's do both and maybe a couple more if they pop up for you.

The step is to declare when you will take action for implementing some additional or new "active income" possibilities. Remember active income? That's where you take steps to find another job, a part-time situation, sell something, and do something that will increase your revenue. Go back to your brain dump sheet and check out some of those ideas. You know, like cutting your neighbor's lawn, selling some of your items you never use, even cut back on the beer and wine.

So now, you have taken two declarations to move forward: declare with gusto what actions you will take and declare how you will take those actions.

The third step today is to shout to the rooftops and declare when you will take action for implementing new "passive income" possibilities. Time is your friend. Say when and then, dance around the room as you declare when you will take action for implementing cost cutting measures. Dance. Move. Get the body involved because the brain doesn't want to be left feeling all alone in this endeavor.

By now you should have some definitive information regarding money - saving, spending, and investing - you will feel more empowered about your personal financial situation as you learn more.

Cindy Skrukwa, in her book, "She Laughed All the Way to the Bank" developed a simple prosperity equation. When applied, you likely can achieve your heart's desire - your goals.

Cultivate positive money attitudes	$
+ Waste less	$$
+ Earn more	$$$
+ Invest wisely	$$$$
+ Protect what you have	$$$$$
___	
Achieve your financial goals	$$$$$$
Achieve your life goals	

CONCLUSION

Today, a few days after your intensive digging and planning and rethinking your current financial situation, I would bet that you might be going through some withdrawal and even anxiety because you are on your own now. It's the end of a journey where I'm with you throughout. After spending time reading and acting upon the exercises here with me, you may still have a lot of negative emotions and feelings about money. You may still find yourself thinking old thoughts that your situation can't be resolved.

I want to support you once more in your own knowing that you are valued, loved and supported. And know that when you make a commitment to a different action step and thought process, providence moves to support you. You truly begin to attract what you want. By continuously addressing your feelings of overwhelm, you can become more resourceful and make better decisions moving forward.

If your overwhelm overshadows your day, you could go into a meditative state, and find that area within that seems to hold a charge of negativity you may still be holding onto.

But I think you already know where that negative emotion is sitting in you. Even though thinking about money makes you feel overwhelmed, you already know to accept yourself and how you feel about your situation. Revisiting the meditations will reduce the energetic charge that your emotions may still have. Once you reduce that charge, it becomes exceedingly easier to make better decisions and clarity which steps to take. You may still be holding some of these more common negative feelings and frustrations.

It's uncomfortable to think about, I understand. Sometimes you'd rather ignore it because you can be so hard on yourself.

You feel overwhelmed even trying to think about money.

These uncomfortable feelings around your finances keep you frozen and feeling stuck.

You may be saying to yourself right now that it's hard to look at your financial situation and you should be better off by now.

You may still be thinking that things shouldn't be like this and you've wanted to change but sometimes it feels out of your control.

It's easy to feel powerless when you think your finances shouldn't be like this.

You're upset you got to this point.

All the ways that you judge yourself, remember that it's safe to give your feelings voice.

All these emotions are already there but now you give them a voice and let them go.

You have the tools, conventional and unconventional to release the stressful energy.

As you address your feelings about money, remember these feelings no longer have control over you.

Awareness brings change. It's safe to give your fears a voice and to finally let them go.

Take a deep breath. When you find that area in your body that is keeping you stuck, revisit it and then do the meditative exercises from to release it.

When you clear this energy, you begin to feel better instantly.

Of course, I am recommending you revisit the elevator and mountain to finally and completely remove the negative energy. Send it into the cosmos and reduce its hold on you.

You can begin to let go of all these judgments that you have around your financial situation. Because even in your current financial situation, you feel calm and centered.

Decide it's safe to let go of these feelings of overwhelm because you are in control.

You are in control as you address your fears and take back your power.

Deep down you know things are changing.

Deep down you know you're capable of reducing debt and making money.

When you come to that place of feeling better, you can begin to look at your financial position from a place of compassion. You're okay where you are because you know things are getting better.

Go through this process any time you need to, and replace your overwhelm with the feeling of power.

You choose to have patience.

You know the power of the single step gets you more centered and clear.

You only need to be clear on the next step. One step at a time.

At every step, you feel more powerful even though your current financial situation isn't the way you wanted to be. But you are willing to take a step forward and focus on how it will become for you.

When you feel better, accepting of your situation, you see new opportunities. You create better habits. You begin to let go of the negative emotions around money as you let go of the judgments and the comparisons. You begin to see your own ability.

Frankly, it was hard to see opportunity when you were overwhelmed but now you have the tools and actions steps in front of you to give yourself permission to be clear this is just the beginning.

Make that commitment to release emotions around money when they come up. You will get clear

The Art of Money Getting

on the limiting stories you have about money and you will begin to let them go. Make room for new beliefs. You can make money in a way that feels good. You have a lot of value to give. Some money flows to you today. And today is a new day. You have the patience you need and you see the opportunities to grow spiritually and financially now. You have planted some powerful seeds this past how many days or weeks you've been reading this guide. Allow these new beliefs to grow. You are clear and calm about your current financial situation because you are now more powerful than you thought. Today is a new beginning and you are ready. Great job today.

MORE BOOKS BY PATRICIA OGILVIE

If you liked this book, you'll love the 1st, 2nd, 3rd and 4th Inspirational Adult Colouring Books in my Series of stress reducers and fun increasers.

Look for my *Bag Lady*, *Marbles* and *Radical Self-Respect* and the public favourite, *Life Lessons for Women* inspirational colouring books for adults.

Plus, look for:

Amazon **Best Sellers**, *Wild Mind: Wild Mind Remembering Last Week's Notes Today*, Revised 2017

And *How to Keep the Ground From Shaking*, 2017

The Most Powerful Person on Earth, Revised 2017

Believe in Magic, 2016

Good Better Best, 2016 children's book

For copies of these books, visit www.auntisays.com/shop/

RESOURCES

Holmes A. (2012) Nature Neuroscience
http://liminalthinking.com/

The Most Powerful Person on Earth, 2011 Patricia Ogilvie

Busting Loose from the Money Game, Robert Scheinfeld

http://auntisays.com/how-to-be-a-financial-hero/

http://whatis.techtarget.com/definition/millennials-millennial-generation

https://china360online.org/?property=understanding-filial-piety

www.ingramcontent.com/pod-product-compliance
Lightning Source LLC
Chambersburg PA
CBHW050118230526
45470CB00004B/1885